FORBIDDEN LOVE

A true story of adoption, reunion and longing

SOPHIA GREENWOOD
WITH HELEN CROYDON

Published in Great Britain by Gadfly Press in 2026

This book is a work of non-fiction based on research by the authors

A catalogue record of this book is available from the British Library

Contents

Dedication:

For my sons - my greatest source of love, strength and courage.

Author's Note

In these pages you will meet two lives pulled apart across decades then thrown, unprepared, into a magnetic, soul-bearing encounter. What follows is based on a true story, told with the intention to explore a phenomenon that, while little known to the general reader, is increasingly encountered in adoption and lost family reunions: Genetic Sexual Attraction (GSA).

We do not tell this story to sensationalise. We tell it to give language to an experience that could be easily misunderstood or judged; to shed light on the wrenching complexity for those who may have encountered it; to examine the psychological attachment processes that underpin it; and to offer readers a humane portrait of the people caught within it.

If you read expecting an easy moral, you will be disappointed. If you read seeking to understand the complexity of human emotion and identity, you may be enlightened.

Prologue, 1964

(Michael and Janet)

Janet was just 17 when she first noticed the handsome yet endearingly shy Michael at a party in inner city Birmingham. He took a while to notice her flirtatious glances across the room. When she saw him move into the kitchen to get a drink, she made her move, following him in to strike up a conversation.

He didn't know what to make of this pretty but unnervingly bold chatterbox taking the lead. Michael was never short of conversation, though he grew uncharacteristically reserved when he found himself talking to an attractive girl. When Janet suggested they exchange phone numbers at the end of the night, he was flattered. Neither were strangers to dating, but as teenagers still living at home with parents, they weren't exactly experienced either.

He called her family's home phone a few days later and they set up their first date - a picnic in a local park. The prospect of a day out was as much a part of the attraction for Janet as Michael was. Having recently finished school, she was biding her time throughout the summer, cramped into a shared bedroom with her two sisters, while she waited for her teacher training to begin – her gateway to independence.

He too was just as eager for an excuse to leave the busy family home. At 18, the eldest of three children with a strict religious upbringing, he was often asked to keep an eye on his younger brother and sister while his parents worked. Unlike Janet, his family lived in a nicer part of town and thanks to his dad's profession as a university professor, he could at least enjoy a house with ample space for them all.

Janet quickly fell for Michael's understated charm. Creative, somewhat dreamy and ever curious about the world, she found him much more interesting than the other boys she had dated, and he seemed modestly unaware of his good looks. Michael was swept along with her. He found all girls fascinating, if not a little terrifying. He'd only become awakened to girls' interest in him over the last year as his boyish looks had finally matured – much later than his peers. It had been a surprise when he noticed girls becoming receptive to him and he soon found that dating was his tool to overcome his shyness.

Until then Michael had never dated a girl for longer than a few weeks. To him, they were light-hearted experiments - pleasant diversions rather than declarations of love. But by the time he met Janet, he'd begun to wonder what it might feel like to be with someone for longer, and to see what lay beyond early flirtations. Among his friends, everyone seemed to be asking, 'Have you ever gone steady?' So, he decided it was something he ought to try. Meeting Janet couldn't have come at a better time. She was lively, attractive and easy to talk to.

Over the next few weeks, they met regularly for lunch or walks. Michael's scatty nature meant he was often apologetically late. To Janet, with all the time in the world, it added to his charm. Once, he fell asleep before their date. They had arranged to meet on a street corner in the afternoon, but he woke up a whole hour after their agreed time. He whizzed to where they were supposed to be, 90 minutes late, and found her still waiting hopefully, in the rain.

Curiosity led them to explore the edges of intimacy but neither were in a hurry to go all the way. Janet had never gone there, and Michael's own experience amounted to a single encounter. One afternoon, during a picnic, they enjoyed a little frolic on a rug laid out in the long grass of one of Birmingham's sprawling suburban parks. When a passerby wandered a little too close, Michael lifted his head and called out, 'Lovely day for it!' They both dissolved into laughter - the kind that erupts from youth, nerves and the thrill of doing something that feels grown-up.

Their romance steadily progressed this way for five months. Janet found herself bowled over by this philosophical, slightly eccentric professor's son from the posher end of town. Michael admired her bubbly, cheeky character. She would ingratiate herself in conversation with absolutely everyone and seemed to know people wherever they went.

When Janet's teacher training began, their meetings shifted to evenings. Michael meanwhile still hadn't found a job and was pondering what he wanted to do with his life, much to his parents' chagrin.

Home life was becoming a strain for Michael. His ambitious parents, anxious for him to make something of himself, pressed him to study harder and settle on a career. They disapproved of his friends, convinced that their son, who they saw to be bright and capable, was slipping because of bad influences. At primary school, Michael had been a favourite among teachers. He was the boy everyone said would 'go all the way to Oxford.' But when he failed his 11 Plus exam, the blow to his confidence was profound. His grades continued to slide through high school, and the label of 'the clever one', which he once wore with pride, faded into feelings of shame. It didn't help that both his younger brother and sister passed the same exam in the years that followed. Decades later, he would learn he had dyslexia and ADHD, conditions barely recognised by teachers in the '60s. At the time though, his parents could only assume the worst - that he was getting mixed up in drugs.

Frequent arguments erupted until his father took action. Unbeknown to Michael, he contacted a brother-in-law in Australia (Michael's maternal uncle) and hatched a plan to send him to Sydney for a year. 'It will accelerate your maturation and give you a new perspective on life,' he announced to Michael.

Michael was stunned. He'd barely even left his hometown, and now he was to go to the other side of the world. But once he reconciled the news, he began to see it as a chance to start over, to put some distance between himself and the tensions with his parents. The thought of leaving his friends and familiar life unsettled him, but he also found some relief in the promise of new, exciting opportunities.

When he told Janet about these unexpected plans, there were tears. Hardly anyone had connections in Australia in those days, and long-distance phone calls were rare, costly and unreliable. Michael pulled away, knowing that staying close would only make the parting harder for her. Still, Janet held on to hope that they would wind their way back to each other when he returned after a year. Before he left, she presented him with a designer pen as a small gesture of love and perhaps a sign of her faith in a future they were yet to define.

A few weeks before he was due to leave, they happened to be at the same party. The emotions of the imminent goodbye got the better of them. Janet suggested they creep into Michael's father's study on their way home. Michael resisted at first, nervous of the wrath of his father if they were discovered. Past experience had warned him that his mother had supersonic hearing! But as with any 18-year-old, it didn't take a lot of persuasion. In the early hours, they snuck into the study in the family basement and had one final passionate hurrah.

They went their separate ways after the party, resigned to the different directions set for them. But there were just enough weeks before Michael's departure for Janet to realise her period was late.

She just knew.

Two days before his flight for Perth, she asked to meet him in a café and there, she dropped her bombshell. They were both aware of the gravitas of this situation. In that era, it was unheard of to raise a baby as a single mother, and unfathomable with their religious upbringing. In those days, terminations weren't easily available, and when they were performed, they were dangerous procedures carrying risk of complications. Even if they did explore this option in secret, with Michael's father so revered throughout the city as a top professor, they were petrified that word would get out.

The other route was marriage but neither dared go there. Michael's head was already full of what adventures lay ahead for him in the southern hemisphere. Dropping it all to marry his first ever girlfriend, in a shotgun wedding, was just not an option. He had little experience of life then, but he had enough to know this would not bring happiness to anyone, including their child.

As if Janet could read his mind, she said quietly, 'Don't worry, Michael. I know having an abortion isn't an option for us, but we could consider adoption. I know girls who've done it.' Her calm, practical words brought Michael some relief. At that moment, it felt like the only path they could take.

In reality though, Janet found she wasn't as detached as she had kidded herself to be. As time went by, the thought of giving up her own baby became harder to imagine and come to terms with. She still hadn't drummed up the courage to tell her parents or sisters. At first, it was easy to conceal her pregnancy with baggy clothes. But as she grew, so did the need to find a solution to her predicament. Overwhelmed by emotions, she shut herself in her shared bedroom and sobbed. When her mother heard her through the thin walls, she pressed the truth from her.

Her mother had little sympathy for what she saw as her daughter's foolishness. Their conversation was brief and practical - more an exchange of instructions than comfort. After some silence, she said, 'You'd better leave before your father finds out.'

Janet tried to talk through options, but her mother had already made up her mind. Within days, arrangements were in place for Janet to stay at a mother-and-baby home until the birth. 'We'll tell your dad you've gone away to work,' she concluded, as if that simple story could tidy away the mess of it all.

That's when it hit Janet hard. Not only did she have to leave her family, friends and the only town she knew, but she now had to face the reality that the baby growing inside her would really have to be given away. To add insult to injury, the father of the child wasn't even here to support her.

The mother-and-baby home was in Henley in Oxfordshire,

a town Janet had never even heard of. Like many such establishments of the time, it was run by a Catholic convent - austere, orderly and bound by silence. The nuns were not unkind, but their manner left no room for warmth. The young women were reminded, in demeanour if not in words, that they were there to atone. Personal questions were rarely asked; in their place they delivered orders for chores – endless washing, scrubbing and polishing. These were meant as both a means for occupation and penance.

There were several other girls in Janet's situation. They all shared a dormitory and since each girl was at a different stage of pregnancy, they all learned what to expect as their trimesters progressed. Repeatedly, someone would reach term, be taken off to deliver and come back days later sobbing. Either their baby had been taken away immediately - if an adoptive family was already lined up; or, they were left nurturing their newborn, knowing their time was limited. All the girls knew that the defeated figure returning from the delivery room would soon be them.

As Janet's due date drew near, the hum of activity around her took on new meaning, each girl's departure marked by the faint echo of a baby's cry, a closed door, a silence that lingered. It dawned on Janet that the moment everyone spoke of so matter-of-factly — the delivery — would soon be hers. And with it came the deeper understanding that deciding to give up a baby and actually doing so were two entirely different things.

***

Meanwhile, Michael worked hard for his uncle in Sydney in his local shop. Pangs of homesickness were frequent and he longed to know what his siblings were doing without their elder brother. It wasn't easy to make friends with a strange accent. More than once people laid into him for being a 'pommie bastard' and he had to fight them off.

For the first two weeks, his uncle took him into their crowded household of seven, with his aunt and five children competing for every inch of space. After that, he was on his own, carrying little more than the twenty pounds in his pocket with which he'd arrived. This was roughly a week's wage at the time. He found a room in a men's boarding house on the outskirts of town and secured a job in a department store in the city centre, commuting in each day by train.

Janet wrote to him, pleading for another way. She asked him to think about making a life together, to be parents to the child she could no longer imagine giving up. Her letters arrived at his uncle's house weeks later, by which time Michael could only guess how things had moved on. Had she changed her mind? Had the baby been born? Even if he did want to go back, he couldn't afford the fare; he had no promise of a future in England; and he would have to face his family. Besides, he still dreamed of becoming an academic like his father. That was a life that felt entirely incompatible with fatherhood. In the end, he worded his reply, insisting that adoption was the only viable choice they had. Seemingly this letter never arrived.

Impatient for a reply, Janet took matters into her own hands and contacted Michael's mother. She revealed her pregnancy and asked outright if the family would support her financially. She was desperate! Michael's mother's response took everyone by surprise. She was a woman of great integrity, guided by her faith but never without compassion. She showed understanding rather than judgment. Reaching out across the miles with a rare long-distance phone call, she offered motherly words of wisdom to Michael: 'If you don't love a girl, you shouldn't marry her just because you've got her pregnant.'

For Michael, they brought a measure of comfort. He had been adrift since arriving in this unfamiliar country, carrying the weight of a decision far beyond his years. The thought of giving up his child was agonising, but his mother's calm counsel helped him see that honesty, however painful, was its own form of responsibility.

Before Michael could write back to Janet, the day came when

her waters broke. The nuns wheeled her into the delivery suite. They were efficient and practical, but there was no tenderness nor compassion for the physical ordeal she was about to undergo, not to mention the subsequent emotional ordeal of giving up her baby.

A healthy girl was born, and Janet called her Emily. She was allowed a first spellbinding cuddle but was sternly warned not to bond too much. 'It's better for the baby if you don't,' The nuns explained.

It suited the convent for the mothers to care for their own babies until adoptive parents could be found. Janet savoured every minute of those precious early days of breastfeeding, holding and caring for her newborn. The morning after the birth, Janet sent a telegram to Michael: '*7lb healthy baby girl born. May 8th, 1965. Name: Emily.*'

As each day went by, the prospect of parting with her newborn became more unbearable. The biological, physiological and psychological process of carrying a baby to term prepares a female's body to nurture and bond with her offspring. To interrupt this process is devastating. When Emily was barely a week old, Janet pleaded with the nuns to help her find a way - any way - to keep her baby. The only possibility, they informed her, would be if the child's father agreed to take responsibility. He would need to be physically present to sign the papers. Without his signature, nothing could be done to prevent the adoption going ahead as planned. Janet listened in silence, the weight of their words settling over her like a closing door.

She poured out her heart in another letter to Michael. One of the nuns posted it for her. But the mail, again, took weeks to wind its way by sea to Australia. By now the wheels were in motion to find adoptive parents.

When little Emily was just five weeks old, the nuns wrapped her up and took her to a vicarage to meet a couple, who'd been identified as a match. It so happened to be the birthday of the potential adoptee mother. Janet was told that the couple had already had one adoption fall through – an experience they found traumatizing, and all the stops were out to appease them. 'They can't be put through the same ordeal again,' Janet was told.

When the couple saw the tiny baby, their hearts melted, and they were allowed to take her home that same day to start her new life in Yorkshire.

They renamed her Sophia.

Janet was sent on her way, by bus, back to Birmingham, her breasts still painfully engorged with milk that was meant for Emily. Bereft, she tried to take heed of the nuns' gentle but ineffective reassurances that her baby would have a better life than she could ever offer as a young single mother.

She threw herself into her teacher training, seeking distraction in study and routine. But she was constantly haunted by the memory of the tiny life she had relinquished, and of the young man she thought she loved but who could not be with her.

Just one photograph exists of Janet holding Emily - in the garden of the mother and baby home, at what looks like days after birth. The image shows Emily in a white dress and wrapped in a white crocheted blanket – the sort a baby may get christened in. Janet has no recollection of when and why the picture was taken.

Chapter 1

A Seed is Sown

1965 – 1983

I always knew I was adopted. I can't say I fully understood the concept, nor what this meant for my identity and how profoundly it may impact me later in life, but I was familiar with the word. As a little girl, I remember being told that I was 'special' and 'chosen.' If ever I brought it up, my mum always said that it made not the slightest difference to her that she hadn't carried me in her womb. She loved me just as if I were her own child.

This was my story, and as I tumbled through childhood, I accepted it as such, with no particular emotional attachment to it. If I was 'special', that was good enough for me!

Growing up, I don't recall feeling sad that I didn't know my birth parents. The truth was, I hadn't really processed what adoption meant – I was too young to realise the enormity of a separation between mother and child. To me, it was simply a history that was recited to me. I might have harboured a mild curiosity about them at times, and I occasionally indulged in fantasies with my friends about one day finding them but, on the whole, I'd tell my school friends proudly that I was adopted. I was far too immature to understand the implications of it for my future emotional and psychological wellbeing.

Yet, somewhere deep inside, I sensed that something was missing - that a part of me was out of reach. I often felt slightly detached from myself, as though I were watching life unfold from a small distance. It was as if my true voice had been muted, and I drifted along with whatever was expected of me.

One of the ways this manifested was a tendency to be a people-pleaser. I remember my parents often praising me for being 'as good as gold'. I've since come to realise that this may have been driven by an unconscious desire to win their approval - perhaps out of a deep-seated fear of rejection - of being 'sent back' to wherever I had come from. I learned early on that assertiveness rarely went down well with them; any attempt to express myself was usually met with reminders to behave and do as I was told. So, I complied. In hindsight, it's clear that I did not fully develop my internal locus of control. My sense of worth and direction seemed to rest almost entirely on the approval of others.

Nevertheless, my childhood was happy enough and my adoptive parents supportive. My father was a government engineer, frequently seconded to different regional sites - defence facilities or airfields tucked away in the Yorkshire Dales or along the coast. Wherever the job sent him, we followed. That meant a new house, a new school, and a new accent for me every two years. My mother was a physiotherapist. It was her true vocation. She loved learning about physical anatomy. But when she married, she was expected to commit to supporting her husband's civil service career and so she gave it up so she could be free to uproot and make a new home every couple of years.

I later learned that my mum did once fall pregnant before they adopted me, but a medication for chickenpox, administered before she knew she was pregnant, resulted in a miscarriage. She didn't manage to conceive again after that.

When I joined the family, my dad was positioned near Ilkley. Between the ages of four and eight, we went to Germany and I attended international school. Then, when we returned to the UK. I went to the local school in whatever town that was.

When I was 11, and about to start high school, my father was contracted to a position near Windsor. By then my parents were growing concerned about the lack of continuity in my education and friendship groups, and decided to send me to boarding school.

I can't remember how I felt about this. I probably didn't

understand what it entailed when I was first told. As ever, I just went along with whatever these adult giants said, without protest. My mum has since told me we went to see several schools, until I expressed that I liked one, but I don't recall choosing or having any thoughts about it.

Strangely, I have few clear memories of my childhood. I can recall the sequence of events, but not details like the rooms I slept in; the faces of friends; the birthdays that must have been celebrated. I've come to see this as an after-effect of being separated from my mother at birth. Though I never consciously processed that loss, I believe some part of me sealed itself off and formed a kind of protective amnesia that allowed me to keep going.

However, one scene I do remember vividly is the day my parents dropped me off at boarding school in 1976, when I was 11. I recall pulling into the car park and lifting my trunk out of the car. In the days leading up to that moment, my mum and I had been busy gathering everything I would need - the crisp new uniform, neatly labelled stationary, and even my first bra, though I hardly needed one! Around me, other girls were climbing out of cars unloading their trunks too, each trying to mask nerves behind tentative smiles. It was the first day of high school and since everyone in my year was new, we were all stepping into the unknown together.

Over the grand entrance to a courtyard was an inscription in Latin which I often think about. It said: '*Ad altiora tendamus*' (Let us aim for higher things).

My parents accompanied me as I was shown to my dormitory and my allocated bed. I was surprised to see the room full of other beds. I must have known it was shared digs, but only now did that hammer home. I also knew that all the girls in here were in the same boat as me, so I wasn't daunted. I was excited to get to know my new friends. Right from the start, I saw each as potential to be the sister whom I never had, and a new family.

I don't remember shedding tears when I bid my parents goodbye – perhaps another telling sign that I experienced disassociation from any memory to do with separation. But I do recall my mum crying, which I hadn't seen before. My dad didn't look that bothered. My mum later told me she cried the whole three-hour drive back to Windsor.

I settled in easily and felt very much at home at this school. It was a co-ed and we all referred to our classmates as 'brothers and sisters'. By today's standards it would probably seem insular because this was the pre-internet era, so no one had access to anything or anyone outside of the school environment. Nor was there any encouragement to explore our individual uniqueness like there is today; There was no focus on discovering and harnessing our innate gifts and talents; No reference to our biological heritage and where our strengths may lie. No one talked in those terms back then.

Academically, I muddled along. Without the daily parental input that I had before, I didn't engage in schoolwork as much as the other pupils. I was always more interested in friendships and sport. I was a natural at both. I joined the athletics, swimming and lacrosse teams, which I thoroughly enjoyed.

Boarding school suited me. It provided an environment in which I felt free to explore who I was, with just the right acceptance of our minor rebellions and the usual teenage hang-ups. I was able to form longstanding, intimate friendships for the first time in my life. Being surrounded by girls my age and observing their differences helped me understand where I fit into the social arena. My confidence grew. I view these years as my first proper phase of independence.

Many of the children came from broken or complicated families. It seems to me that boarding school provides, for many parents, a dumping ground for kids who are perceived to get in the way. Of course, many send their offspring with the best intentions for a better education, but more often, I've observed that it's because there are complications at home. When my mum met some of my friends during holidays, she would often comment that I seem to have attracted a lot of 'broken friends'. But what did she expect? She sent me to a breeding ground for them!

This happy chapter of my life was cruelly cut short after three years. Aged 14, my dad was promoted and offered a job in Stockholm, Sweden for three years. My parents decided that given the length of this contract, I should leave boarding school and go with them for the remainder of my educational years. I wasn't performing academically very well and they concluded a smaller school, under their watchful eye, would make me work more and play less. This seemed to be the single basis for their decision, rather than them missing me. If they'd expressed the latter, I may have taken the news a little better.

I was horrified. I felt I truly belonged in that school. I had little connection with my family over the previous years; we spoke every Sunday on the phone, and I went back during the holidays if I hadn't been invited to stay with one of my friends. So by then, my schoolmates felt more of a family to me than my parents did.

When I told my friends about this plan to move me to a foreign country, they were shocked. It felt like losing a sister for all of us. I remember one of my friends wailing, 'I can't believe you're leaving us Sophia!' In our dorm that night, we got out a world atlas and looked up where Sweden was. I told them it was a country 'full of fields', because that's what my parents told me. What they actually said was 'full of fjords'!

A week before I was due to leave school, my grandfather was taken to hospital having had a stroke and I initially refused to leave early to visit him because I didn't want to cut short the last precious week I had left.

I was very close to him however, even though he was my grandmother's second husband. So, when the gravity of his condition hit me, I did of course go to the hospital with my parents. I'm so glad I did. The stroke was serious, and he was lying unconscious in the bed when we arrived. I remember feeling distraught at seeing him so poorly. He was such a kind and jolly man, who always made me feel special and loved. I held his hand and I remember saying, 'Grandad if you can hear me, squeeze my hand.' And he did! It was a beautiful moment. I will never forget how special that felt and how I clung to his hand as my parents told me we had to go. I wanted to stay by his side all night. But visiting hours were over and rules were rules. I never saw him again.

Life in Sweden was challenging as I grieved the loss of my boarding school sisters and brothers. The international school my parents found was small, with intimate classes and very little emphasis on sport. Looking back, I can see it must have been an adjustment for them too. Suddenly they had a fourteen-year-old - all hormones and uncertainty - move in with them after years of enjoying life on their own.

But, it did force me to get my head down and work hard in the run up to what were then called O-levels. It was a beautiful country with long, hot summers and snow in winter. I became really good at ice-skating and cross-country skiing – or *langlauf*, as they call it there.

During those formative years, my curiosity about the part of my story that had always felt like a fairytale began to deepen. I found myself wondering more and more about where I had come from. With friends, I would muse whether it might ever be possible to trace my birth parents. Every so often, I'd make tentative enquiries about what such a search might involve, though I never took it further than that.

After my O-levels, aged 17, we were due to return to England. The inevitable question arose from my parents – what was I going to do with my life? There was minimal access to career advice back then, so my knowledge of the abundant paths one could embark on in adult life was very limited.

When I asked my mum if she had any ideas, she told me about the career she had chosen. She was inspired to become a physical therapist thanks to a kind and entertaining physiotherapist who tended to her broken arm as a child. This sparked an interest in anatomy and helping others. Her dedication to her profession had seen her work in hospitals, private clinics and even government offices, which is how she met my dad. I'd never heard her speak of her past like this, and I could hear the passion and animation in her voice. So I decided, with no real idea of what I'd be good at or enjoy doing, that I'd give physiotherapy a go too! This was another typical characteristic of mine - following where I was guided, exercising no independent will of my own. My mum did warn me that there wasn't much money in it unless I could find a way to get out of the public sector and work for a private practice. But that didn't register. I probably thought if it was good enough for her, it was good enough for me.

We researched vocational colleges from our temporary home in Stockholm and sent off several applications. I was accepted by more than one and I chose a college in Twickenham on the outskirts of West London because I liked the look of the cobbled streets and the river and the prospect of shopping in central London!

And so it was that I followed her path. I had to wait to turn 18 before I could start the training. I always had an affinity with children, so I took a job as a live-in nanny for a couple and their three children in London.

At the time, I felt lost. I still missed the friends I'd been torn away from at boarding school and any new friends I'd replaced them with were all now in Sweden. I didn't feel close to my parents. They supported me but I could never open up emotionally to them about anything. When I entered this bustling family of three as a nanny, it was an eye opener. Seeing how another family interacted made me realise that I had missed out on a connected, happy family life that was clearly possible to enjoy. I found it fascinating to see inside someone else's family life. Both parents had full-time responsible jobs and the three children had each other as playmates on tap. I was in awe of them at first, but enjoyed being a part of their lives. I didn't take great care of myself back then. I didn't eat healthily or prioritise sleep, but the mother (my boss) was very kind to me and rather took me under her wing.

I asked her one day how she coped with running such a busy household with three children under the age of nine. She told me that she was a born-again Christian and her faith gave her strength and joy every day. I was fascinated by this and asked her what being born-again meant. I was at the age where I was pondering the meaning of life, and had often hovered on that perennial human question: Is there a guiding force in our lives?

'How can I know there is a God in the way that you do?' I asked her.

'Jesus died for our sins and through him, you can know God. If you invite him into your heart, you will be saved.' She replied.

'Is that it? I just ask him?'

'Just get onto your knees and say a prayer and acknowledge that you're a sinner, and you'll be born again in God.' She replied with conviction.

She was a mature woman and always seemed so sure of what she was talking about. I remember thinking, 'Maybe this is what I'm looking for - a meaning and a purpose to life that's been alluding me.'

That night, alone in my room, I knelt by the bed and offered my first conscious prayer to 'God', whoever or whatever that might be. I asked Him (I suppose I imagined a 'him' because most people did then) to come into my heart. What happened next would set me on a lifelong path of spiritual curiosity.

I remember a vast, gentle, almost luminous presence filling the room. I sensed a beam of light, or perhaps only something my mind created, but it was enough to take my breath away. Whether it was imagination or something beyond hardly mattered; what stayed with me was an unmistakable assertion that something beautiful had happened.

The next morning, the world seemed different. Colours were sharper; the air felt fresher; trees looked greener; birdsong sounded crisper. I carried a strange new clarity - as though a window had been wiped clean and I was seeing life, for the first time, as it was meant to be.

That experience opened a quiet awareness in me that there may be a hidden dimension to life. I began, from time to time, to speak in prayer to whatever higher presence might be listening, asking for a little guidance along my way.

After that, I joined a prayer group and began reading the bible with my boss in her home bible study group. Everyone seemed so full of love, always with the best intentions and great generosity of spirit.

'Something amazing has happened. I've been born again! I'm going to get baptised.' I told my parents when I next saw them. But I was dismayed to be met with their nonplussed expressions. They curtly told me that they had baptised me as a baby, and there was no need to get born again. When I told friends or colleagues about my newfound faith, they also rejected the idea as nonsense so I stopped talking about it and kept it to myself.

***

When my physio training finally began, I loved it. It took three years to qualify with a Diploma in Physiotherapy (MCSP). For the first six months it was mostly theory. Then I got to don my medic trainee hat and do regular stints at a hospital – I could be placed in any ward from orthopaedics to neurology. It's common in a busy medical environment to step in to help when resources are short, so I'd often find myself doing duties above and beyond my physio training, like bed baths and bottom-washing!

Working in a hospital throws you into a tough world, especially for one so young. I was exposed to gravely ill and injured patients and I stepped up to the role as best I could considering my tender age.

One day, around a year into my training, as part of a placement on a maternity ward, I somehow ended up being present during a birth. I was not prepared for the overwhelming emotional reaction it triggered in me. To witness new life emerge from the safe cocoon of the womb, drawn from darkness into light - the mother caught between agony and awe – was both sacred and primal. In that moment, I was awakened to the symbiotic bond between mother and child - a connection woven from equal parts pain and love. As I looked at the newborn before me, so fragile and unguarded, I was struck by their vulnerability. This tiny being was entirely dependent on another human for love, safety and the ability to survive.

The experience opened in me something that had hitherto been unaddressed – my desire to know where I came from and why my mother had given me away. Suddenly the image came to me of her giving birth to me – how could she have handed me to someone else after going through this? It dawned on me now that perhaps she hadn't wanted to give me away. Perhaps she was forced to? In which case, was the pain of childbirth made worse by knowing that she'd have to hand me over to another mother in a clinical exchange? Or, did she want to give me away because something in her life prevented her from caring for me? Had she loved me? Wanted me? The mother I watched now in this hospital room was praised by the nurses. I momentarily imagined my own mother and what she might have gone through. Had she felt guilty and shamed for having me? And what about my father? How had he felt? Whatever the circumstances, it must have been pretty awful for them to give away their own baby, I thought, as I watched the mother cradling her newborn with a radiant smile on her face and the father beaming proudly by her side.

These questions had always been bubbling away within me, but I'd never dared confront them before. I knew now that the answers had huge implications. If it were the case that my birth mother had loved me, but just couldn't keep me for some reason, and had always wondered where I ended up, that would change everything about my self-identity!

Everyone in the birth room was joyful but I felt overwhelmed by the deluge of thoughts that had just unexpectedly taken over my conscious mind. Why was I given away? Where was my biological mother? Unexpected tears stung my eyes. I tried to fight them, but I couldn't so I left the room. That evening, I couldn't stop reconstructing my own birth and thinking about my birth mother. I went to a friend's house and poured my heart out. 'Where is she?' 'Does she ever think about me?' I cried.

That was when the seed was sown - I must try to trace my birth mother.

Chapter 2

Too Much Too Soon

1984 - 1989

As moving as that encounter in the delivery room was, I still tiptoed around the idea of tracing my birth parents. Each time I thought about it, I feared the emotions it might stir in me.

One day, I got as far as looking up adoption in the Yellow Pages. That doorstopper of a book was the first point of research for everything back then. There were several agencies I could call, and I wrote the numbers on a piece of paper and left them on my bedside table in my single student dorm. They stayed there for weeks. When I did drum up the courage to call – on a payphone in our corridor, I asked the receptionist for more information on what the process would be. She ran through it: I'd first have to fill in a form, which they could post. Then I'd have an appointment to speak to them, then they'd come to visit me in my home for a formal interview, then they would start researching to see if they could trace a record of my mother that matched the information I provided. It sounded very complicated. They sent the form in the post, but I didn't even get close to filling it in. It felt too overwhelming to confront the emotions that may ensue, and so I decided to leave the idea well alone. Clearly, I wasn't ready.

The catalyst that would change everything came when I was 23, four years after that delivery room experience.

I was, by then, a fully qualified registered physiotherapist. Fresh from a nine-week casual job on a children's summer camp in the USA as the on-site first aider, I secured my first ever permanent job at a rehabilitation unit in a hospital in west London. I lived in a single dormitory in a building dedicated for junior medical staff. A few weeks into my job, I got chatting to a nurse colleague in the staff room on our coffee break. Somehow the conversation veered to a question about whether we had brothers and sisters.

'No, I'm an only child.' I replied.

'Me too. I'm adopted.'

'No way. Me too!'

Now we had a connection that only another adoptee would understand. We exchanged loads of information on each other's backgrounds, knowing we had a shared lens through which we viewed our childhood. Then she said, 'Actually, I recently found my birth mother.'

My heart skipped a beat. So it was possible to do this, without everything caving in. 'No! How?'

'I went to this agency and they found her. It was easy. It turns out she lives up the road. We met up and it was amazing. I see her all the time.' I listened in silence. 'You should try too. I'll give you the number.'

The casualness with which she described this news and outcome gave me reassurance. I looked at the piece of paper on which she'd scribbled the agency's details. It was called NORCAP, which stood for National Organisation for Counselling Adoptees and Parents. (NORCAP since stopped trading in 2013 and its contact register was taken on by the Adoption Services for Adults).

That night I knew something had changed. I was spurred on to start my search again - properly this time. The next day, again from a payphone, I called NORCAP, with much more conviction than last time. They took my details – date of birth, birth name, place of birth and any other crucial details which could help identify my biological mother. 'Someone will be in touch.' They said, as if I were booking a consultation for a house viewing.

In 1988, there was no national register of adoptees. Voluntary intermediary agencies like NORCAP allowed adoptees and birth relatives to register their willingness to be contacted, but the system was voluntary and not centralised so it was a bit of potluck whether two relatives would be reunited. Then contact could only happen if both parties had separately come forward.

If I had started my search for my birth mother three years later, it would have been easier because in 1991 the government introduced the Adoption Contact Register, a national centralised database for adoptees and birth relatives to express their formal wish to connect.

A few days later, I drummed up the courage to tell my mum and dad that I was considering finding my biological parents. I remember the moment in their living room after I'd gone over for Sunday lunch. We'd never talked about this before, but my instinct always told me they wouldn't welcome the idea, so I was nervous. I didn't realise just how much resistance they would have, however.

'We don't want anything to do with that.' My mum snapped.

Then my dad added the sting in the tail, 'She didn't want you. We were told that she could never come looking for you, even if she wanted to. If we'd known the law was going to change, we would not have adopted you. If you want to find her, that's up to you, but we don't want to know.'

'Ok. Sorry.' I replied. Being pushed away like this was common. But like always, I didn't fight back. I felt like the guilty party for upsetting them. My relationship with my parents was a strict – albeit supportive - one. I always felt there was no room to share my views because whenever I did, if the views differed from theirs, I was dismissed or shut down. The disassociation with my true desires kicked in, as it always did in situations like these.

I continued my search behind their backs and it was never mentioned again. I now understand that they feared losing me. I was their child and just like I was wary of the emotions a reunion might disturb in me, so were they. I later learned that shortly after this chat, my father approached a female welfare officer at work, who had some dealings with adoption counselling as part of her job. She was a modern thinker for her time and advised my dad to support me in my search, and that this was now recommended for the benefit of all concerned. So, he had clearly gone away and thought about my plight, but ultimately, he couldn't face embarking on my journey with me, or maybe he felt like he would be betraying my mum.

A week or so after I gave my details to NORCAP, they called to arrange a preliminary interview at my home. At this stage, they just wanted to check that I was of sound mind for such a charged life event, that my intentions were positive and that I wasn't looking to enact revenge on a parent for giving me away (it happens apparently!). A nice gentleman showed up at my flat, and we drank tea as I relayed all the information I had stored up about my biological mother. I knew where the convent was, and I knew my mum's first name, but not her age. I knew she had given birth in a convent and that she had called me Emily, but I didn't know anything about my father. The case worker took notes and said the agency would contact me if they found a strong match. Then off he went on his merry way.

I cracked on with life, not giving it too much thought. With such scant information about my mother, I didn't expect much. Perhaps I subconsciously hoped nothing would come of it, and then I could just carry on and not have to merge the real story about where I came from with the one I had told myself.

Ten weeks later – the time necessary to process my application and do whatever detective work these agencies need to do - I received the fateful phone call.

'We'd like to invite you to our offices in London as we have some news for you.'

'What news?' I asked hopefully. But they wouldn't reveal any clues. I arranged an appointment the following week, getting a train from Wimbledon to central London and then the Tube to Tooting, where they had a pokey office. A colleague from the hospital came with me. I didn't know her that well, but I gladly accepted the moral support.

I was shown into a dour meeting room with no windows,

where a prim woman sat with reams of notes in front of her. 'We've looked into our records; we've matched everything up and we can confirm that your mother registered with us 15 years ago.'

This news felt like the proverbial bolt out of the blue! My story about my beginnings, which I had carried for years in my imagination, was now leaping off the page in full graphic detail. The woman who gave birth to me is alive and out there somewhere, looking for me! She has a name – and she had left a contact number! It was wonderful and shocking all at once. Suddenly, after all these years the reality hit me that I had two mothers.

This was the best outcome I could have hoped for. I had imagined that if my birth mother had registered with an agency, hoping to find me, that it would have been more recent, perhaps reflecting on life as she grew older. But fifteen years indicated that she had been thinking about me throughout my life. She had held on to me. She probably hadn't wanted to give me away. The enormity of this thought, and what it meant for my identity, put me in floods of tears right there in the consultation room.

To my surprise they handed me her name and phone number there and then. I later learned that it is not best practice for agencies to do this so quickly. They should ensure adoptees receive up to six months pre-reunion counselling. Not only that, I was also quite unceremoniously informed that I had a half-brother, aged 17, and a half-sister aged four.

I left the meeting in a daze, buzzing with equal part excitement and apprehension. It was such big, ecstatic news. But it was also news I realised I was drastically unprepared for.

What now? Would I be able to pick up the phone and speak to my birth mother for the first time? What would I say? Would she be pleased to hear from me? What if someone else answered the phone? All these questions flooded my mind on the train home. The colleague I travelled with did her best to be sympathetic, but it felt strained because I didn't know her that well and I was struggling to reign in my wild emotions.

When we parted ways, I stopped to pick up food shopping

near home, operating on autopilot. But I burst into tears in the aisle as the gravity of today's news bedded in. The unexpected twist that I had a half brother and sister added to the heavy processing load.

The next day, I went to my best friend Alice's house, who I knew from boarding school. We waited for her two young children to go to bed and then with her support and encouragement, and a glass of wine, I picked up the rotary telephone receiver and traced the numbers around the circular dial. My heart was racing, and I felt the sting of welling tears – tears of trepidation more than anything.

A female voice answered.

'Hello, Is this Janet?' I ventured.

'Yes.'

My heart jumped. How to introduce myself had been a dilemma I'd contemplated many times in my mind and hadn't yet reached a conclusion. Simply saying the words: 'Hello, I'm your daughter' felt like a strange betrayal to my adoptive mum.

'Hi Janet. My name is Sophia. I think I'm your daughter.'

There was a pause, and then I heard 'Sophia…? Emily!' and she fell apart with joy. She shrieked and sobbed and we ended up talking for two hours, starting with how we found each other through the agency. My friend left us to it as we shared details about our respective lives with a glass or two of wine. Having had no pre-reunion counselling, I had no idea what to expect from this call, how it may leave me feeling, or whether it was recommended to set boundaries of any sort. I felt like a character in a TV drama.

She told me straight away that she had wanted to keep me. She kept using the phrase 'at 17, I had no choice'. She was told that a secure (and married) couple could provide for me in a way that she wouldn't be able to. There was no discussion about support for single mothers. Adoption was the popular fix in those days, with little consideration for a mother's devastating grief, nor the trauma that the baby would no doubt experience from separation.

It was clear that she remembered everything about the ordeal in minute detail. This was the biggest story of her life. Making contact after all these years was as momentous for her as it was for me, but our experiences, memories and feelings after the separation had been very different. For her, finding me - her long lost daughter - was explosive for her heart. She had loved me at birth and had never stopped thinking about me. But for me, although I knew I had a biological mother out there somewhere, I had no conscious memory of our bond. I didn't feel any love for this lady. She was a stranger to me, even though I felt her deep maternal love for me. It was a surreal situation – talking to this newcomer in my life as if we knew each other; sharing intimate information about our lives, hearing declarations of her love for me, when obviously she didn't know me. I didn't really know how to reciprocate.

She had a Midlands accent and I remember thinking that was strange. I hadn't met anyone who talked this way before – I'd been to international schools and a boarding school and hadn't been exposed to provincial English accents. The contrast accentuated a difference between us. 'I've thought about you every single day. Every year on your birthday I sent you my love…' she repeated, more than once.

We arranged to meet as soon as we could. With her based near Birmingham and me near London, we decided on a pub outside Milton Keynes as a mutually accessible and neutral meeting ground. I would also get to meet my half-brother and sister.

There were a few more phone calls in between, and two weeks later I set off for the grand reunion by car. It was a really hot day. There was no sat nav then of course, and I had to keep stopping to look at the map, going off course several times. When I arrived, I was hot and bothered.

I remember vividly scouting out the restroom because I wanted to freshen up and gather myself before greeting them. As I walked through the lobby bar area, I spotted three people standing by the bar – a woman with dark hair and two children. I instantly knew they were my relatives. I saw the resemblance between them and myself immediately, even from a distant glance. I had never seen anyone who resembled me before, and it sent my heart racing.

I carried on walking, hoping they hadn't recognized me yet. When I emerged from the bathroom, primed for the big moment, they set eyes on me and from their faces it was clear that they also instantly registered who I was.

I hugged my birth mother first. This was a moment I had imagined so many times. She was warm and welcoming and it was lovely, but it also felt a bit odd. On the one hand, I knew we were related and I was thrilled to have physical contact for the first time with my birth mother; but on another level, she was so unfamiliar to me. Her perfume, her shape – it meant nothing to me. It was a strange dichotomy to stand before the woman who gave me life but yet feel no belonging. Then I hugged my 17-year-old half-brother, and my four-year-old half-sister. All three of us shared a mother but each had different fathers. Bonded by genetics, yet so unfamiliar with each other's energies.

I didn't have much of an appetite so I ordered a Caesar salad. 'Oh, I love Caesar salad too!' Janet exclaimed and ordered the same. There were lots of other 'me too' interjections from her that lunchtime as she grasped onto every single similar trait as a sure sign of our DNA match.

There was no shortage of conversation. We exchanged information about ourselves and marvelled at the series of events that had led us all together after all these years. It seemed that fate had indeed had a hand in orchestrating this reunion. When I learned that her father was an osteopath and her mother a nurse, I could not help but ponder the odds of me being drawn to a similar profession. Then she mentioned that my birth father dreamed of becoming an artist when they courted. Drawing has been a passion of my own - surely this was more than mere coincidence? Was there a genetic propensity passed through the ancestral line that had found expression through me? That my adoptive mother was also in the caring profession of physiotherapy was also intriguing. It made me return to my simmering existential curiosity: Are there any coincidences or is everything fixed as it should be, for reasons that we are unaware of until we have the gift of hindsight?

Janet was widowed. She had retired from teaching and rented out rooms in her house to students for a trickle income, which she loved, and spoke fondly about all of them, clearly showing her natural maternal instinct. My half-brother was at college studying for A-levels.

The meeting flowed so well that Janet suggested we go to her sister's home, who lived nearby. She had an outdoor pool, and we spent the afternoon in and out of it, me in a borrowed swimsuit from Janet. The symbolic familiarity of a daughter casually borrowing an item of clothing from her 'mum' was not lost on us. I unexpectedly ended up staying the night. It was late and the long drive home, after such an emotional day, seemed out of the question. My mother's sister - my biological aunt - was a nice lady and obviously excited by our reunion. I didn't pick up on any resemblance or genetic connection with her though. I think I was so consumed with the novelty of being with my birth mother, that I didn't even compute that my aunt was also a blood relative! The whole meeting was pleasant, but at the same time surreal. At times it felt like I was observing the whole scene, as if I were an actress in a movie, without feelings.

At 23, I was not equipped to deal with such emotional complexities. My excitement at meeting these people was overshadowed by sadness as I became aware of the chasm of lost time. It exposed a void that no amount of time or wishing things were different could fill. I also felt simmers of anger, and a sense of victimhood. Why me? Why did everyone else have straightforward linear connections with their families? It wasn't fair. Meeting my biological relatives should have felt like finding the missing jigsaw piece that I'd been looking for my whole life, but somehow it felt like a phantom piece – it didn't change my reality of losing my mother after birth. It didn't magically 'complete' me as I perhaps thought it might.

I already had a mum, who I loved, and who had been there for me throughout my childhood; who'd dressed my bleeding knee; soothed me when I was feverish. The role of 'mother' was filled. Where would this other mother fit into my life, when it is culturally established that we only have one mother? Maybe that's how experienced counsellors could have helped me process these arising feelings, which were confusing, and hitherto unknown.

This first meeting was followed a few weeks later by a second, and we had lots of phone calls in between. My birth mother's feelings of love and loss ran deep, and she was always quick to pour her heart out about what our reunion meant to her. Many times, she repeated how she'd carried her love for me - her relinquished baby - for twenty-three years. I too had carried the idea of love for her - my unknown mother - but as part of my story, not because I had any conscious memory of my short time with her. For me, it didn't translate to conscious, affectionate love. My relationship with her was, by its very nature, intimate whilst, paradoxically, not intimate. It was so very confusing.

It was a challenging time grappling with this inner dialogue and myriads of resulting emotions. To complicate things further, I couldn't discuss this with my adoptive parents. Given their reaction when I told them that I was considering my search, I set up all these meetings without their knowledge. The guilt, knowing they would be mortified; along with Janet's keenness to pursue a relationship as mother and daughter, just confused me even more. I lost a lot of weight, torn by loyalty to my adoptive parents and the developing relationship with my birth mother.

Six months after we first met, at Christmas time, Janet announced she was having a big party, and invited me and my then boyfriend.

We drove up to Birmingham, where she lived, and booked into a B&B. I thought it was just a Christmas party, but it soon became clear that this had been arranged with me in mind, as a kind of celebration of our reunion. She had invited all her friends and extended family so they could all 'meet Sophia'. It was clear how excited everyone was about me being there. Everyone was asking me questions and telling me how wonderful it was for Janet that she'd finally found me and that the resemblance between us was striking.

Unbelievably, Janet and I turned up in almost identical dresses without having conferred about our outfits, which didn't help with all the dramatic declarations of fortuity.

'I don't believe it!' She exclaimed when we greeted. 'We even have the same taste in clothes.'

She bought me a necklace engraved with my initials as a Christmas present. Then she presented me with a vinyl record of *Eternal Flame*, signed by Cilla Black – a household name TV show host at the time. Janet was a big celebrity-follower and she had somehow managed to get a letter to Cilla, with our story of reunion, and got her to donate her signature. She said the words to this beautiful and poignant song always made her think of me. Her eyes welled up when she recalled the chorus.

> *'Close your eyes, give me your hand darling, do you feel my heart beating? Do you understand? Do you feel the same? Am I only dreaming? Is this burning an eternal flame? Say my name, sun shines through the rain. A whole life so lonely, and then you come and ease the pain, I don't want to lose this feeling...'*

I too had listened to it many times and had found it extremely moving.

Although the gesture was touching, and it was lovely to discover my half-brother and half-sister were keen to get to know me, the whole evening was intense – not to mention an eye opener for my rather shy boyfriend!

In the weeks leading up to the party, Janet had rung me almost every day for long chats, evidently wanting to get as close to me as possible after all the lost years. She too was probably struggling to deal with intense emotions that she wasn't equipped to process.

Her love was for the relinquished baby called Emily. All that unexpressed love, pent up over many years, was being projected onto me, but I was now an adult called Sophia. Of course, I didn't understand this then, I just recognised that I was struggling to manage the relationship.

After the party, I made a conscious decision to distance myself and tried to resume my normal busy life as a physiotherapist. Then, later that winter, came another situation that threw me into further turmoil.

Janet called me, all excited. 'Turn on the TV!' she cried. I tuned in to ITV and there she was - a pre-recorded clip of her talking to a chat show host about our story of reunion! It turned out she had told her story to a woman's magazine for one of their 'real life' features, and was now appearing on a chat show to be interviewed about it. It was all too much. Why hadn't she discussed it with me first? I expressed my concern that my parents might see it. We had a few cross words and it ended with me snapping at her to 'please just leave me alone!'

And so, about a year after our first contact, our communication abruptly ended. But little did I know that Janet had by now contacted Michael and told him I had come looking for her. The story of my biological family reunion was far from over.

Chapter 3

1964 – 1989

(Michael and Janet)

Michael never came home from what was supposed to be his one-year working holiday in Sydney. He instantly loved the outdoor lifestyle and the sense of space, and for the first time in his life he was earning money. Back home, all he could see for himself was pressure to find a respectable career; what that would be, he didn't have the slightest clue! He was still reeling from failing that 11-Plus exam that his whole family were convinced he'd pass with flying colours. Then he had got a lovely local girl pregnant. It was easier to stay put, rather than have to return to the scene where everything had seemingly gone awry.

He revelled in his newfound autonomy, but it wasn't plain sailing by any means. After his uncle told him that his stay of welcome was up and he was on his own, he had to pay for a boarding house. To make ends meet he got a job in a department store. He detested it because it was way too formal for his free spirit. One day, on the one-hour commute from work, he fell asleep on the train and woke up at the end of the line. The train was already in a siding, and he had to climb out of a window and over the tracks. An official caught him and accused him of being a vandal!

He lived hand to mouth, earning just enough for rent and food. His first step up came when he got a job in sales and stunned his managers by quickly surpassing the performance record. Unfortunately, his boss still wouldn't employ him full time because he was convinced that this energetic character would soon get bored with a such a monotonous job. Instead, the manager suggested that Michael should go to university because he was clearly a very intelligent young man.

This planted a seed, but Michael couldn't even begin to think about how he would fund further education. He carried on looking for the best-paid ad hoc jobs. Door-to-door sales seemed to be the thing where he had the most success, and soon his healthy commissions meant he could afford to rent a place on his own.

On his 21st birthday, for the first time in his three years of living in Australia, he ventured out of Sydney. He and a friend went on a road trip, driving the whole breadth of the country to reach Perth on the west coast – a trip of nearly 4000km. They stayed with the friend's friend. This friend's friend's girlfriend made a beeline for Michael, and they ended up in a relationship lasting three years. That was the end of life in Sydney for Michael and the start of a new chapter in Perth. Now, the prospect of returning to the UK seemed even further away.

Twice Michael got close to tying the knot with his new love, but he always had a sense that he was destined for something else – something he just couldn't put his finger on, but that meant he couldn't commit to marriage. He still felt a niggling incompleteness about those failed exams; still wanted to shed his label of the nomadic older sibling. One day, he might study for a degree and go back and show them all!

One of his sales jobs inadvertently put him on the path for another career though - one more fitting to his entrepreneurial, creative nature. He was tasked with selling subscriptions for family photoshoots, knocking on doors and convincing families of the nostalgia value.

He noticed how many properties had maintenance issues that needed attention and it sparked an idea. He could drop flyers through letterboxes while on his rounds, offering odd jobs like fence repairs, paintwork, guttering, roofing. Michael wouldn't do the work himself, but capture the demand, pass on the opportunities to a circle of vetted tradespeople and take a 20 percent cut. When his batch of test flyers successfully brought in calls, he formalised his idea into a small household maintenance business. In the pre-internet world, it was a forward-thinking business model – operating as middle-person funnelling business leads.

Michael struck up a friendship with one of the regular workers on his books and picked his brain endlessly about the trade – how to judge a job, what things cost and the red flags. Before long, he had learned all about the sector and was running his own thriving business. Within a year he had reliable enough income to buy a sports car: A super-cool Aston Martin that was his pride and joy.

He continued this business into his mid-20s. But still, he remembered the message instilled from childhood that is important to have a 'real' career. As successful as his maintenance business was, it would never pass the litmus test for his conservative family back home. His father's academic credentials always hung over him and after much research into what prestigious academic qualification could utilise his natural creative flair he decided on architecture. He applied to all the architectural schools back home in the UK and was turned down by all of them. Some said he was too old, and some said he didn't have the mathematical qualifications nor enough examples of technical drawing. He widened his search to Australia and eventually his local university in Perth accepted him, on the proviso that he acquired the relevant mathematics and physics grounding by attending night school first. Architecture was already as long a course of study as medicine, so this would be a long haul but he was committed. He also resigned himself to the fact that this would make a return to the UK increasingly unlikely.

During these years, thoughts about the baby he had given up were never far beneath the surface. As he grew older, the awareness of his child, carrying his DNA, existing somewhere in the world pressed more heavily upon him. He began to feel an unspoken burden weighing on him - something between sorrow and guilt. He considered the possibility that, somehow, one day he might be able to find her.

He tried to suppress these emotions and told no one that he had fathered a child until he was 42. On what would have been the 23rd birthday of 'Emily', he was at a loss to explain his melancholic mood; so, he confessed to his girlfriend.

'I've got a terrible secret I need to tell you.' Then he found himself sobbing and sobbing. Something he'd never done in front of anyone as an adult before.

After this, he told another person – a friend - and then once it was out in the open, and he found people were supportive and sympathetic, he considered the possibility that one day he might be able to find her somehow.

Shortly after that, he organized his first trip back to the UK to see his family. He hadn't seen them in 25 years. He didn't tell his mother. He wanted it to be a surprise. In the days leading up to his visit, he had a vivid dream that he met with Janet. It was so strong that he told his girlfriend that it was more like a premonition than a dream. She reassured him that it was probably just the all-to-be-expected nerves about revisiting the past, peppered with some buried, but needless, guilt.

But he couldn't forget this dream. His intuition told him that there would be something more to this trip, that it may uncannily lead him to his lost daughter. He decided he would not try and engineer such a meeting with Janet but would go where fate led him. On his flight, he had a few days stopover in Thailand. His premonition grew so strong, that he was compelled to call a friend in Perth to discuss it.

When he landed at Heathrow airport, he called his mum announcing his imminent arrival, who was ecstatic. Once she'd stopped whooping for joy, she asked, 'Did you tell anyone you were coming?'

'No, why?

'Because strangely, Janet called this morning asking where you now live, and if she could have your contact details. Apparently, she has something to tell you.'

Michael should have been stunned but strangely, he wasn't. It was as if his premonition that they would meet had prepared him.

A few days later, once settled into the embrace of his delighted family, he took Janet's number from where his mum had dutifully noted it. 'Are you sure this is a good idea?' His mum queried. She'd remembered that the last time Janet contacted the family, she asked for financial support – an act of desperation to keep her baby.

'It will be good to put this whole thing to rest. I still feel bad about it. And it wasn't her fault.' Michael replied.

They met at Janet's house. There were tearful embraces. Janet was clearly bursting to tell him her news: Their relinquished daughter, Emily, had found her, and they'd met! She effused how wonderful she was. She'd gone to a 'great family high up in the civil service'. She went to boarding school and 'speaks really well.'

Then the sting came. Janet refused to give Michael their daughter's details. 'I don't know if it's right or if she is ready,' she said. She failed to reveal to Michael that 'Emily' had since told Janet to back off. Michael didn't press her. Perhaps she harboured some leftover resentment of how she perceived he abandoned her, Michael thought. Yet he had faith that this was destiny's plan unfolding. He didn't know exactly when, but he felt an imminence that he would meet his daughter, and so he graciously accepted Janet's decision to withhold this information for now.

Long after Michael returned to Australia, he continued writing to Janet exchanging news and asking her to reconsider giving him their daughter's contact details. After three months, Janet had a change of heart and acquiesced, only then revealing that she had been renamed Sophia.

Chapter 4

A Message From the Past

1990

A few months after my communication ceased with Janet, I received a knock on the door from the postman. I opened a package containing a VHS (an old-fashioned video tape). Wrapped around the tape was a piece of paper with a cartoon-like sketch. It showed a man sporting wings, flying through the sky over a world map with an arrow following the line from Australia to England. He had a bunch of flowers in one hand and a suitcase in the other. A speech bubble above him read: 'I hope she's not cross.'

My heart skipped a beat. Could it be…? I looked again at the envelope. The airmail sticker and the Australian stamp confirmed my conjecture: This was from my birth father.

A flurry of thoughts streamed through my head. He must have got my address from Janet. He must still be in Australia. Who is he? What's his motive? I was full of curiosity, but my dominant emotion was, for some reason, one of irritation. 'How flippant,' I thought. 'Cross' wasn't an emotion that came to mind when I thought of my adoption, and it seemed presumptuous of him to pre-empt my state of mind. Now, looking back, I understand how hard it must have been for him to know what to say. He was trying to be sensitive to how I might feel, hearing from him out of the blue. I was, however, impressed by the cartoon drawing. It was genius. I'd never seen such a refined sketch in real life like that, only in magazines or newspapers.

I couldn't face watching the video alone. And anyway, I was on my way to work. I saved the moment and took it to Alice's house the next day to play it - the same friend whose house I was at when I called Janet for the very first time.

Unlike when I called my birth mother, I didn't feel the same nervousness and anticipation at hearing his voice. I was detached this time. 'Come on, let's see what this is.' Alice encouraged after we'd poured a glass of wine and put the VHS tape into the machine. It felt more like we were about to embark on some light dramatic entertainment, than the great unveiling of a personal mystery.

On the screen appeared a slightly grainy image of a man in his 40s in beige shorts and a white linen summer shirt, looking into the camera and introducing himself. 'Hi Sophia, I'm Michael and I'm your father.' It began.

Neither of us had seen an amateur home-video recording before. Camcorders were very new then. He was on his driveway outside a modern and spacious house. Everything was bright and sunny. I noticed jasmine growing in the bushes beside him. It looked like an exotic place.

Despite the bright sunshine, he didn't wear sunglasses. He looked directly into the camera and told me about his life. This was his house in a suburb of Perth; he was an architect; he loved photography and art, and enjoyed these creative pursuits in his spare time. He showed me the street he lived on and pointed to where he headed for walks.

Then he got to the heart of the matter. He started to tell me how sorry he was for giving me up, how he had no choice, how things were so different in the 1960s. He seemed friendly. Deep down, I knew this recording was meant as a sweet gesture - an attempt to show me who and where he was. But I was still struggling to process my emotions after the experience with my birth mother, and this felt to me like he was making an assumption - that I would embrace his approach without any warming up. I, like many adoptees, had experienced a full range of emotions over my birth parents – dreaming about meeting them one day; feeling resentment that they abandoned me the next. This man's playful attitude, on the screen in front of me, seemed to portray that he could just waltz into my life in a jovial way and this irritated me a bit. In hindsight, I realise he was trying to be engaging, but at the time I became defensive. To me he was a stranger and this home video, filmed with a camcorder - a flashy bit of tech at the time - seemed slightly over the top. When the ten-minute recording was over, I threw the tape and the winged man in the bin in a fit of pique.

I now realise, having watched TV programs like *Long Lost Families* – a reality show featuring families being reunited - that concern about being forgiven, and a desire to explain are universal themes among long lost relatives. This was what was behind Michael's words, 'I hope she's not cross'.

At the time though, I didn't know what to make of it. I didn't have any older, wiser mentor to guide me through this emotionally charged time. I just got on with my life and chose to ignore it. But a few weeks later, I received another letter from Michael. This time I softened, acknowledging that his intention was caring. I wrote back and thanked him. I gave him enough details to satisfy him that I was ok – my career and where I lived, probably. But other than that, I gave him scant details about who I was.

I don't remember how long the response took but I do know that it was March 1990 when I received his first phone call. I don't recall giving him my phone number so I can only presume that Janet did.

'Hi Sophia, this is Michael. I wrote to you. It's your father.'

Despite my surprise, I couldn't help thinking that I liked the way he talked and handled himself. He asked me lots of questions. At first, I was cool, politely answering but not being open and generous with my conversation.

I found myself thinking he was lovely to listen to, with a kindness behind his words. It felt like he genuinely cared. He spoke beautifully with soft dulcet tones. And he was so articulate. I told him that I travelled a lot when I was growing up with my dad's job. I went to boarding school, and then to an international school in Sweden.

He told me how he had no choice but to give me up all those years ago. He was young, scared and unable to cope with the situation. 'I've thought about you so much over the years.' I remember him sighing.

He didn't gush with love as Janet had. We chatted about all sorts. He never seemed short of anything to say. It felt easy. He was engaging and made witty comments that made me laugh.

After that phone call, he started to call regularly. Slowly we built up trust. I softened a little more with each phone call. The energy between us felt different to the intensity emitted from my birth mother. It felt more equal somehow. But it was still hard because I endured the same battle that I had when forming a relationship with my birth mother – hiding the communication from my adoptive parents.

In Michael's next letter, he sent a photo. He was on a beach with his arms outstretched. He looks fun, I thought. I looked for some resemblance of me in him but couldn't see any. Soon our calls became every other day. I was now totally at ease with him. I started to notice how uncannily alike we were in our humour and tastes and views. We just 'got' each other in a way I had never experienced before.

In fact, we got on so well it started to feel like we had a psychic connection. Just as I would think about him, he'd ring. I was still living in the shared medics' accommodation in Wimbledon. There was no communal lounge, and it did feel like I was slumming it a bit. The only phone I could access was the payphone in the corridor. Often the other residents – mostly young women like me - would answer and come to find me. They all knew who he was. 'It's Michael again!' They'd say cheerily. I would sit in the dark hall chatting for ages, unperturbed by the possibility of being overheard.

In my personal life, I was single and dating like any other 20-something. There was one particularly passionate ski holiday romance with a gorgeous Austrian ski instructor. We skied and drank *glühwein* on the slopes and he was all for staying in touch and me going back to Austria to visit, but a long-distance relationship didn't appeal to me, and so we soon lost touch.

About two months into our phone chats, Michael said, 'I think it's time we met, don't you? Perhaps I could come to England and stay for a couple of weeks?'

I was really excited by this idea. I had absolutely no qualms about it being awkward or intense. By now, Michael felt like a close friend. I was so at ease with him; I even felt I knew him more than my own adoptive dad. I recall saying to my adoptive dad as a teenager, 'I wish I knew you better dad.' His reaction was to shake his head and say, 'You don't want to go there love, you might not like what you find.' And that was as far as we got. But Michael was open and happy to share details about his childhood, his two siblings and the experiences that had influenced his character. He'd talk about psychology and philosophy and the universe and cultural evolution. I'd never met anyone as intelligent and educated in my life. He was well read on world affairs, and he'd tell me all the geopolitical highlights, yet without being opinionated, and never once making me feel inferior. One topic I was fascinated in was his take on human cultural evolution and whether culture affects the DNA that is passed down the generations. We'd philosophise about this for hours.

His flights were reserved for mid-July for a two week stay. Since he knew I had a single room in a shared communal building, he asked if I would investigate nearby hotels.

Along with the hotels, I also enthusiastically researched activities to do, places to sightsee, exhibitions to visit. It was ages away yet, but our excitement mounted. 'How about booking a little holiday? To get away from life's distractions and really get to know each other.' Michael suggested spontaneously on one of our phone calls.

I knew how much he loved to travel, and how much he loathed English weather. Living in Australia meant he didn't have opportunities for short-haul travel to new cultures, so this didn't seem at all out of the ordinary. He was aware that I didn't earn much as a junior physio, so he graciously suggested that I chose somewhere and he'd take care of it, without outright announcing that he'd pay.

I happily took on this research mission. I phoned a travel agent the next day – which is what everyone did pre-internet! I told them our dates, and that we wanted sunshine and something modest. I was very price conscious. The agent came back with an outstanding value all-inclusive deal in Turkey.

'I found this lovely place and it's only £500 for the week for both of us.' I said excitedly when we next spoke.

'Great!' he said. I needn't have checked with him. He was always easy going about everything. He just let me take charge and went along with whatever I suggested. He never struck me as flashy or particular about tastes. He made me feel good about what I'd found.

Before he arrived, I had a mini drama, which ended up with a fortuitous outcome for my living arrangements. Our dormitory accommodation got burgled – it happened while I was on the ski holiday getting to know the handsome Austrian instructor! Everything went and so I had to apply for a new house to live in through the hospital where I worked. I ended up getting first dibs on a newly furnished place, which I would share with just two other housemates. It had its own lounge and even all the necessary crockery and cutlery in place. I moved in before the other two so there would be a short window where I had the place to myself – right when Michael was due to arrive. Now proud of my new, airier place, I told him that he didn't need to look at hotels, he could stay with me, on the sofa in the lounge if he would prefer that.

That may sound like it would be intense, but I was excited about having a place to myself for the first time ever. At 24, I was happy to share my space and preferred to be with people than alone. We had been talking for such a long time, this just felt right. It would have felt odd if I'd packed him off into a hotel, especially as this trip was to spend time with each other. Plus, he was taking unpaid leave from the architecture practice where he was employed, so I was happy to save him money if I could, which could go towards our holiday in Turkey.

As the day approached, I had no qualms about telling anyone about the upcoming highlight of my summer. My friends and colleagues were excited for me too. No one ever expressed any reservations about my newly found father staying with me, or us going off on holiday together. If my friends had any concerns, they didn't voice them.

Perhaps if my parents, or another responsible adult, were behind me, someone may have said, 'Do you think it's a good idea to have someone you've never met in your personal space for two weeks?' But such concerns weren't in my peer group's consciousness, nor mine for that matter. I was just intrigued and went with the flow.

I chatted happily to my clients about how I was soon to meet my biological father for the first time. On my last shift before he landed, I remember one of them wishing me luck for the big reunion.

Little did I know that day was to change my life forever in unimaginable ways. It was to set me on a journey of conscious awakening and an earnest search for how and why things happen to us in our lives.

Chapter 5

Meeting Point

1990

It was the height of summer when Michael flew to the UK from Australia. The night before he arrived, I went to Alice's house. Fortuitously, she lived near Heathrow. We set our alarms for 5.30am – all the flights from that part of the world arrive ridiculously early – and she drove us to the airport. Both of us were buzzing with anticipation. I was so grateful to have the support of a friend, especially one who was familiar with all the events leading up to this reunion.

I felt nervous as we walked into the Arrivals Hall, hardly remembering it was so early. Other than the video of him showing me his house and street, we'd only seen one image of each other, so I worried I may not recognise him!

I spotted an overhead sign: 'Meeting Point'. I smiled inwardly, feeling the metaphorical significance of this phrase too – meeting a significant new part of me. Nothing after this point was foreseeable. Just like when I met Janet, I was stepping into the unknown. Like then, I felt a heady mix of apprehension, reluctance and excitement. I hadn't coped particularly well with the intense new relationship with my birth mother – how would I manage this one?

We spotted each other at exactly the same moment. He was holding a camcorder and scanning the throngs of people in the hall. 'Sophia, Sophia where are you?' he was saying quietly to himself.

He looked up from the view finder on the camcorder and our eyes met. 'Sophia! Hello at last!' he smiled warmly before quickly adding, 'You don't mind me filming, do you? I wanted to capture this momentous occasion on film.'

I wasn't expecting that, but I didn't mind. I hadn't really experienced being filmed before. 'Not at all,' I said, and we had our first hug. I noticed he smelled fresh, even though he'd endured a 22-hour flight. Jazz aftershave, I later learned.

I remember thinking how his face seemed oddly familiar. He was well-dressed and I remember sensing a lovely energy about him. As we chatted, never was there a sense that he was a stranger. He felt like someone I had known, but hadn't seen, for years. After all our long telephone conversations it seemed I knew him well.

Alice drove us back to her house. It was still only 8am and her two young children and husband were now up, busying themselves with breakfast and getting ready for school. We stood in her tiny kitchen, trying not to get in the way, chatting. Michael stood by the sink and seemed to take the hustle and bustle going on around us in his stride. He engaged playfully with the children as they ate peanut butter on toast, putting them at ease and making us all laugh. But we were both a little self-conscious and clearly on our best behaviour. I could tell by his cautious conversation that he was thinking, 'I wonder what she's thinking of me?'

By 9am, Alice and her family had emptied out to go to their respective office, school or nursery and left us to it.

'Shall we go into the garden?' I suggested, noticing the lovely sunshine which had appeared. In my nervousness, it hadn't even occurred to me to offer him a drink, and he considerately didn't ask for anything.

We moved to a small garden table, and I sat down feeling remarkably relaxed but recognising the same surreal vibe as when I met my birth mother. 'How do you feel about the camcorder?' he asked again.

I shrugged. I was sort of aware of it, but it didn't bother me. So, he got it out again and let it roll. It's apt for me to explain a little about this video here before I go on. When Michael returned to Australia, he spent evening after diligent evening, editing the footage captured during our time together. He hooked up the machine to his VHS video player and kept pressing *play – record - stop*, to capture the highlights he wanted to save. Somehow, he cut a selection of our favourite music to it, which would have been a technology feat in those days. The result is a beautiful film that he called, 'Meeting Sophia'. To this day, it is still one of my most treasured possessions.

I mention this video here because some of the scenes and conversations I recall in these next chapters were prompted by this precious recording.

There I am, with my cropped brown hair, leaning back on my friend's garden chair with my feet up, smoking a cigarette like I was putting the world to rights with an old friend. Michael pulled out a miniature bottle of duty-free Cointreau. 'I got this on the plane. Shall we toast this auspicious moment?'

'At 8 in the morning!' I exclaimed, smiling. 'Sure, why not!'

We started to chat about our lives. I told him about a medical trial I had recently taken part in for £100. I took an anti-acid pill for a week and then had an endoscopy. He made a joke about my insides all being in order, and it made me laugh.

Soon our conversation turned to the chain of events which led to this meeting - how my nurse friend gave me an agency number; how a social worker came to visit me at home; how the official broke the news to me in their office that they'd traced my mother. 'They handed me a piece of paper and it had my birth name on it. Then, underneath, it said adopted and my new name, Sophia. It was a major identity crisis!' I ended.

Then once more, he relayed his story of how, in 1964, he felt he had no choice. As a teenager, he wasn't aware of his options. He lived in a place halfway around the world and it wasn't so easy to get flights then.

'I'm sorry I never got to read you a bedtime story.' He added.

I was taken aback by this. It was a strange thing to hear. But

I reminded myself that the man in front of me was the father who *would* have read to me as a child, if he'd been around. Yet he didn't feel like my father, and that's why the words coming out of his mouth seemed incongruous. There was no clarity on what our roles should be in a situation like this one. I had no benchmark as to what was appropriate. Because Michael and I had built so much connection already through our phone calls, I decided this comment wasn't inappropriate – it was just a tender, reflective expression, sitting before his long-lost daughter, and being reminded about all the fatherly moments he'd missed out on.

I giggled to try and avert the slight awkwardness and then we directed the conversation back to our life histories. He told me how he started his own odd jobs company in his 20s. 'I was completely self-taught and I set it up because I was sick of doing shitty sales jobs and making other people money.' He relayed, and I couldn't help admiring his chutzpah.

It seemed to me like he had a natural talent for spotting what people need. He told me many funny stories about the strange jobs that homeowners demanded and the unexpected lives of some of the workers on his books. Then he told me about the Aston Martin which he had treated himself to – a much-enjoyed symbol of his success.

But, he relayed, he always felt like there was something more to achieve. He'd always been told he was bright – possibly destined for Oxford so when he struggled with his O Levels and A Levels, it was a blow to his self-esteem. 'I was the only one out of my siblings to fail the 11 Plus. Now I know I'm dyslexic and have ADHD but these things weren't well-known about in schools in those days.' He explained.

As the son of an eminent professor, he became driven to make something more of himself. He told me about the difficulties applying to architecture school without maths or physics A Levels, and how he had to complete two years of night school to get the base qualifications needed.

For two years, he ran his property repairs outfit by day and attended college in the evenings. In a trying test of his tenacity, he had to drop back a year because of a fire in his apartment. He lost everything, including his income. The stress of it meant he struggled to keep up with his studies. But he persevered and finally, he got his grades, aged 30, and duly started his architecture degree alongside a load of 18-year-olds. He spoke with passion, and I was full of admiration for his determined spirit.

Suddenly I became aware of the heat of the sun and realised that we had been here in the garden chatting for hours. We hadn't eaten, nor even had a cup of tea. I suggested we go to a popular pub in Barnes Green, not far from my Wimbledon flat. We got into my white Ford Fiesta and drove the 30-minute journey.

A few weeks earlier, I had met one of Michael's Australian friends. He was visiting the UK and Michael had put us in touch. At some point, I drove him somewhere and he was blown away by our unexpected similarities, 'You even drive like Michael!' he had remarked. I think what he meant was that we were both nippy drivers! Clearly this had been reported back to Michael because in the car now, he said, 'Wow, you really do drive like me. How is that?!'

We enjoyed a traditional English pub lunch in the beer garden. The familiarity and ease between us deepened by the hour. The more we talked, the more it transpired that we shared similar views, had the same sense of humour and oh, how he made me laugh.

I loved his upbeat attitude. He was interesting and novel. He listened and seemed always engaged. At 24, I had always been attracted to older, dynamic, articulate men - with a perceived wisdom of the world, but I hadn't met many of them. Michael was all these things. And he was funny and quick-witted. For anyone, his company would be endearing. To me, as a woman, it was particularly so. He made me feel safe and made me laugh. It felt nourishing to chat with him.

I kept searching his face for signs of me, but I couldn't find any.

He had bright, blue eyes and mine are hazel. He had a strongly built nose, which I don't have. He was fair. I am dark.

After lunch, we walked to The Green. The camcorder came out again and a plane flew above us. Michael turned the lens to the sky to capture it. 'That was you a few hours ago.' I commented.

'It was. I was looking down and wondering where you were.' He replied, watching the plane as it flew out of sight. 'Would you like me to show you how to throw a boomerang?' he continued, producing one from his bag.

I started having a go, throwing it using a technique he coached me through – aim it at a point just above the horizon, tilt it slightly to the right, and throw it at around 45 degrees right of the wind. Sometimes it came back to me, and sometimes it didn't, and I kept running across the scorched short grass to retrieve it.

'I've tried to teach this to so many people and no one has picked it up so quickly.' He remarked, clearly impressed. My heart warmed. He must be thinking that this is a sure sign that I'm his daughter!

When I tired of throwing, I asked, 'Can I show you my skill?'

'What's that?'

I did a handstand and walked on my hands – my party trick! Our video shows me suspended for almost a minute with a perfect C-curve in my spine. He was very impressed. I joked that I could try to teach him. 'Err no thank you, I'll leave that party trick firmly in your domain!' He laughed.

Eventually, he started to look tired and I suggested we go back to my home. No doubt he needed a shower and a rest.

At the door to my flat, Michael hit the record button on the camera again. 'Welcome to Sophia's house.' He said, continuing the running commentary from our first day together. We went into the garden, camera still rolling, and I opened the garden shed and joked to the camera, 'This is Michael's room, he hasn't tidied it as you can see!'

'Yes, it's very soiled,' he said pointing the lens at a bag of soil in the corner, which we found hilarious.

We carried on like this, bantering and laughing and that evening I cooked a delicious chicken dish. The camera again on me, shows me shimmying to music, throwing herbs and shallots into a big bubbling pan as I showed off my culinary skills. We chatted some more, before Michael succumbed to sleep at 10pm. I insisted he have my bed instead of the sofa, even though he graciously tried to object. I thought it better that I take the living room so that I had freedom to use my flat in the morning in case his jet lag called for a long lie-in.

But I was too charged to sleep straight away. I lay on my sofa – which would be my bed for the next week – trying to process what just happened. I was blown away. Perhaps if I'd thought to call a friend then, it may have helped me articulate my feelings. All I knew was that I had an amazing day with this fascinating man, and he felt nothing like a father!

I had no context for these feelings. No 'box' to put them in. On the one hand, it felt distinctly like flirtatious energy, but on the other hand, it surely couldn't be because we're related. Yet, this connection felt *nothing* like I had with my adoptive dad. These couldn't be daughterly feelings. Nor could they be flirtatious feelings. So, what were they?

As I lay alone in my lounge going over the events of the day, I dared to admit that what I was feeling was akin to romantic attraction. We'd put no boundaries on our feelings. Perhaps we should have done, but we didn't. Why would we? How could we? Nothing had prepared us for the possibility that we could find ourselves attracted to each other. From his perspective, how could he relate to me as his child? He didn't know me as a child. He hadn't raised any other children either. He was meeting me for the first time as a woman.

My feelings turned to frustration, even slight anger, as I realised that I'd been seeking this sort of comfortable, easy, natural connection with a man my whole adult life, and yet here I was feeling it for the first time with the one man I shouldn't be feeling this way about!

Chapter 6

The Kiss

1990

I had a fitful night of dreams sleeping on the sofa that night. My first thought when I awoke was to wonder how Michael had slept in my single bed. Then, my confusing thoughts from the night before flooded in: How could it be that I set out to meet my father, to complete the jigsaw of my life, and he ends up feeling nothing like a father, but instead, like a man I am inexplicitly drawn to, but in a completely unexpected and disconcerting way? I kept thinking I should have similar feelings for Michael to the ones I had for the father who had brought me up from five weeks old - whom I loved and respected. But my feelings for Michael felt nothing like the daughterly relationship with my birth father.

I could see into the kitchen through a little serving hatch in the lounge. I heard movement and looking through the hatch, I did a double take. Michael had wandered down in a white, extremely short dressing gown which ended at the top of his firm thighs. 'Not seen that before. That's a bit sexy!' I remember thinking, before quickly berating myself for such an inappropriate thought.

Trying to snap myself out of this loop, I dismissed my thoughts as heightened emotions, mixed perhaps with a smattering of admiration for this charming, funny, intelligent older man whose storytelling and repartee I was really enjoying.

We had three days at my home before our overseas trip, and we spent them completely engrossed in each other's company. Michael presented me with a gift - a long, country style raincoat by the brand *Driza-Bone*. Here in the UK, this was known as an upmarket, classic label but apparently in Australia it was common on the high street. It was clearly expensive, but the classic look wasn't me at all. I was a free spirit and dressed casually. This seemed frumpy and too old for my style. I tried to be polite, but as we got to know each other, he registered that it wasn't really me and spared my embarrassment by saying he'd take it back with him to return it.

As each day went by, we became closer. We seemed so in tune with each other, intuitively understanding what the other was saying. Every conversation resonated on some deep level that felt like a homecoming - the finding of, and the merging with, one's soulmate. I felt so happy but at the same time a sensible part of my head was screaming at me, 'Hold on! You didn't feel this level of intimacy with your birth mother. Is this right? Why are you feeling all giddy and soft inside?'

I was sure I detected mutual feelings from Michael. In fact it was hard to deny the unacknowledged attraction between us, bundled together with confusion.

Regularly, our conversation would touch on the circumstances that led to my adoption and Michael would relay again how hard it was for he and Janet; that they had had no choice. He told me of the anguish that grew over the years as he started to question where in the world his daughter may be. It was clear that whatever burden I had carried my whole life from mother-baby separation, Michael also bore some kind of paternal equivalent.

By the time our departure day to Turkey came around, we were completely absorbed in each other and must have looked, from the outside, like a happy couple going about their business.

I drove us to Gatwick as the sun was rising for an early flight. On the car stereo, we played a tape of an album from Australian artist, Paul Kelly, who Michael had introduced me to.

When we landed at our destination, we were met by the tour company and boarded a coach to our apartment. With every step of our itinerary completed successfully, I breathed a sigh of relief.

Having planned the whole thing myself, I was eager that it was an appropriate standard for this successful architect!

A pretty English girl in the tour company uniform gave us a history lesson from the front of the bus and again Michael captured it on camera.

'In Turkey, they don't have much. But they are very proud of what they have.' She opined in a cut-glass plummy accent. 'If you have a wardrobe in your room, consider yourself very lucky. My room just has hooks. The Turkish toilets are different to ours. You may find them quite basic. They are starting to install some western ones, but why should they? This is their country and why should they change?'

We were sitting up front and Michael kept making funny quips, which made her laugh. After she finished her spiel, he started asking her where she was from and how long she'd worked for the company. She smiled wryly and looked at me nervously from the corner of her eye. I noticed in myself a slight discomfort – surely I wasn't jealous?

Most of the other tourists were dropped off at big hotels. Our accommodation, however, was a small guesthouse on a cobbled street run by two brothers, who welcomed us in with bitter, black Turkish tea. It was modest – a bit pokey - but the architecture was beautiful and the view from our room over the dark blue, luscious sea dotted with islands of rock was breathtaking. It was clear I'd selected this through the lens of a price-conscious junior NHS worker. I had selected a 'studio room' presuming this meant two beds in two separate rooms. But now I saw the two beds were in one large open space.

'This is great! What a view!' Michael exclaimed without a blink at the bed situation. Again I felt relief. He was so easy-going. One of his most admirable traits, I was learning, was his ability to get on everyone's level, and his disregard of status and materialism.

Each morning, one of the brothers in the guesthouse brought breakfast to the room so we could eat on the balcony looking out on the most stunning view of a dark blue, rippling sea. We heard the loudly broadcast call to prayer every morning at the same time and this would cue Michael into talking about human cultural evolution and the diversity of cultural norms around the world.

All the time, I could not shake the discomfiture that this felt nothing like a long-lost father-daughter relationship should, but more like two people falling in love!

On the afternoon of day two, we explored the coastline, walking over rocky enclaves. I kept dipping into the sea. I'm a confident swimmer and I was showing off my skills, jumping in off the rocks, screeching louder when they got higher. Around the next corner, we stopped at a bar in a rocky bay. From our seats on the veranda, we could hear the waves lapping. My bikini was still wet, and my matted short hair was dripping down my shoulders. I was enjoying the hot sun warming me. Live music was playing and both of us felt complete contentment.

And that's when it happened.

I can't remember who leaned in first. We probably both did, in synchrony. I remember his piercing blue eyes getting closer to mine, and I could smell his pheromones mixed with sand and sea. The kiss felt so tender. So sweet. So *right*.

'This doesn't feel wrong, does it? Why doesn't this feel wrong?' He whispered.

The boundaries we had tried so hard to observe were now crossed. But there was no jolt of disbelief. No guilt. It was just like having a kiss with someone you love. It felt so right that it was hard to get our heads around the fact that it should feel wrong.

'There's a part of me that's never been certain whether you truly are my daughter.' He said quietly. 'We never had proof, no paternity test done.'

This was probably the worst thing he could have said. While we knew deep down this was highly unlikely, those words sewed a seed of hope that we might somehow be free to be together, and so, we foolishly allowed our intense feelings to engulf us.

The electrifying kiss between us left us both giddy and tentatively wanting more. We watched the beautiful sunset over the water holding hands, both deep in our own thoughts, reliving the moment that just changed everything. We were alert to any arising feelings of guilt or regret, and ready to address them then. But they didn't come. Why did we feel such powerful magnetism between us? Why didn't kissing each other jolt us into shame or repulsion?

We wandered back to our apartment hand in hand, feeling a whole new level of intimacy, and a whole space in us open up to each other. My heart was racing and my tummy was doing those funny flips – that sensation when you think about kissing the one you're attracted to.

When we got back to our room, there was a frisson of anticipation in the air; we both felt the powerful desire for physical closeness engulf us. We stood there in our room, holding each other for the longest time, nestling into the now familiar smell of each other and when we finally drew back and looked into each other's eyes, we both knew that the other wanted this and our silent consent was given.

Making love with Michael was the most beautiful, tender and loving intimacy that I had ever experienced and almost brought tears to my eyes. This union didn't just feel like a sexual act carried out, as is often the case to satiate a physical desire; it felt more like a union of souls, a dance, a symphony of love expressed for the other with tender adoration and gentle human touch.

We lay in each other's arms, enveloped in that beautiful peaceful feeling that washes over you when you find yourself thinking 'there's nowhere else I'd rather be', and then we drifted off into a dreamy sleep as the fan whirred and the crickets chirped.

The rest of our holiday could not have been more idyllic if I'd planned every minute in advance. Everything flowed. If it weren't for the *Meeting Sophia* video, I may have doubted my memories as rose-tinted. But hours of real-life footage don't lie. The grainy amateur pictures show us enjoying truly halcyon times. We're seen lying starfish in the shallow waters of a pebble beach as the swell lapped around us. We're seen sitting on the deck of a boat, the wind in our hair, gazing worry-free at mountains in the distance. We're seen frolicking at a water park, diving off a waterfall, and me holding a handstand on a diving board. We're seen on our balcony eating fresh bread and soft cheese joking how 'awful' the view is (being sarcastic obviously!). How oblivious we were then that what Michael captured on film was the unfolding of a most unexpected and portentous love story.

The days were long, hot and luxurious. The balmy nights were spent under the clear night sky, eating the local, rich cuisine and chatting with the friendly waiters and shop owners. In every frame, not a care in the world can be detected.

At lunchtimes, we'd banter and chat in whatever restaurant we found ourselves in. Michael had so much to say. He'd comment on something going on nearby. Or make cultural observations or dissect theories on human cultural evolution. In the evenings, we went to beautiful candlelit bars and listened to live singing. Everywhere we went, Michael chatted to everyone – other tourists, shop owners, boat captains. He was entertaining, clever, funny, kind.

He even made me laugh when I got sick with 'Turkey tummy', which I suspected was from a slightly off melon. For two days, I was – at the risk of too much information – on the toilet a lot! But it didn't bother me that he had to be privy to these unladylike moments. In any new relationship in times gone by, I would have been so embarrassed, but I wasn't with him.

When I was feeling better, he came into the bathroom putting on a hilarious exaggerated French accent and said, 'Would madame like to join me for dinner, now she's recovered from her *Mal d'melon*.' He was just naturally witty.

One scene shows us in the back of a carpet shop, chatting to the owner, sipping tea. We'd been mooching the streets when a stall holder tried to sell us something. Instead of shooing him off, Michael started jesting with him. Next thing, we were lying sideways on their Kilim rugs, pouring tea, and stroking their dogs, all because he just connected with them. Yet he was always mindful of me, including me in his repartee. I felt like my own expressiveness and humour was developing as a result.

Another time we hiked up a hill to see the ruins of an old stone cottage. We were approached by sweet, old ladies chewing herbs like gum, trying to sell us their wares. Michael stopped and looked right at them. 'Look at these ladies. There's so much life in them!' He said, totally tuned in to their authentic selves. He started talking, asking about the herbs, play-acting with smelling them and making the ladies laugh. He always gave his full self to people.

When we managed to pull ourselves away from the old ladies, after buying some herbs, we reached the ruins of the abandoned stone cottage. Out came the camcorder again, and never short of energy, Michael went into acting mode.

'Welcome darling, to our new home.' He bellowed, with grand hand gestures as he glided into what was once the front room of the cottage. He continued going through each tiny door of the dilapidated building. 'This is where I keep my chamber pots.' He said, moving into a small area, and I gleefully tuned in to him, making it a double act.

'This is some jam I've made,' I pointed to some old, mouldy jars on a shelf, 'And this is my overnight bag,' I laughed gesturing to an old stained bag hanging on a hook. We continued like this before we had to stop because we were laughing so much.

One of my favourite memories is making friends with a nine-year-old girl. We were walking through another market when the little girl, with short brown hair like mine, tugged at my sleeve. She looked like I did at that age. She was trying to sell us perfume. Without a blink, Michael crouched down to her level and asked her to spray some perfume on me as a test. Shyly, she complied.

'Repeat after me,' said Michael, 'I can smell you.' The little girl reciprocated. 'I smell nice.' Micheal said. Again, she repeated him. 'But I smell NICER!' 'But I smell nicer,' the little girl copied, giggling in delight. She had limited English, but Michael somehow communicated with her for a good ten minutes. She became so enamoured with us that she asked her mum on the stall if we could come back the next day 'for cake'. We gladly accepted, and at exactly the same time the following afternoon, we revisited her family's stall, with a present – a tube of chocolates gift-wrapped in brown paper. She was all dressed up in traditional clothes, eagerly waiting for us. Her mother and little sister were with her, and they beckoned us into the back of their family stall where they brought out traditional Turkish cake and served it with jasmine tea. I'm in the video asking her to teach me how to say thank you in Turkish, (*Teşekkürler*). It was not easy to pronounce! We wrote to this little girl and her family after our holiday. She and her mum wanted to hear about our country, and we sent them photos of English countryside.

I was so taken by how Michael could engage effortlessly with people - how he gave them his undivided attention and never judged. That's what he gave me and that's what everyone wants.

He taught me to be observant of other human beings and their unique qualities. Already, on the holiday, I felt myself becoming more open – freer to express myself without constant self-censoring. One sign of this evolution was when I challenged the guesthouse owners to an arm wrestle. This was another of my party tricks! All the heavy lifting I did with my physiotherapy work, alongside lots of swimming had given me strong biceps. It came about as we bantered with them when they brought breakfast to our balcony. I won – or maybe the brother let me! But whatever, I never would have had the confidence to instigate such a thing before.

I also admired how Michael was always fixing things. This was one of the things I observed during our first days together. In a restaurant one windy day, our sun umbrella kept falling over. Instead of accepting it, like I would have done, or asking a waiter for another table, he set about finding something to tie it down with. In our apartment too, he'd changed the layout of the room to make it more spacious. These sound like small things, but it piqued my interest because I never thought out of the box like this. My upbringing had taught me that you have to accept everything as it is – you can't move a sun umbrella to your table if it isn't already there.

Another time, he booked the most in-demand restaurant in the town. We had to pre-order our fish in the morning, and they went to catch it that day. They brought it to our table and cooked it in front of us. I would never have thought we could even get into a restaurant like that; I'd never experienced such bespoke cuisine.

When we tucked in, he raised his glass and said, 'Here's to love, human cultural evolution and your sweetest dreams.' It was the most romantic moment I'd ever experienced.

But beneath this bliss, bubbled the unsettling thought that this couldn't last. At times this expressed itself as insecurity. Like, when we went to a restaurant with a topless dancer and instead of being impressed by Michael's warm, open conversation starters, I got a bit jealous. I suppose it triggered my underlying unconscious fear of rejection.

On the penultimate day of our magical trip, we sat on a rocky ledge overlooking a bay. Both of us were thinking it, but until now had not articulated the pain of separation that was to come. I was dressed in just a peach swimsuit. It was me who broke the silence, overwhelmed by a wave of sadness.

'Fuck, what are we going to do?'

'Indeed. What *are* we going to do, Sophia?' he repeated wistfully looking out onto the bay.

We did of course discuss the morality of our unexpected love affair. We were both intellectually aware that by blood, as far as we knew, we were father and daughter, and yet on an experiential level, we had no shared life experience to give this relevance. We came together as man and woman, meeting as strangers. There was a complete absence of any social conditioning that would have resulted from a shared family history. No family legacy to influence the way we interacted with one another.

I had set out to meet my biological father, to find out about my roots and instead, I had met and fallen in love with Michael, the man, not Michael, my father. That such depth of connection could even exist was a revelation to me. I had never felt anything like this. He opened in me a wonderland of feelings. We were so alike in so many ways. We read each other's thoughts constantly. We connected fully and completely.

You may find yourself judging us at this point - perhaps thinking that while I was only 24 and naive, Michael should have known better. However, from our endless conversations about this over the years, it's now clear that he did not have the capacity to switch his feelings off. He, like me, had been carrying years' worth of anguish surrounding the act of giving up his daughter. Guilt, secrecy, confusion and immaturity at the time; then the subsequent years of speculation about where and who his daughter may be. The culmination of this emotional alchemy when we finally met is too complex to even attempt to analyse.

When we returned to London, Michael had another five days before his return flight. It was inevitable that he extended his stay. He asked for a further two weeks off, without pay, from the architect firm where he worked. We went to Holland by train and ferry and danced the night away in Amsterdam. Then we explored the city by boat and bike. I'm seen in the *Meeting Sophia* video, sleeping soundly in the train carriage as we returned. Then we drove up to the Lake District. We played Turkish music the whole way from an album we bought on our holiday. We went hiking in the hills. When it rained, we laughed and walked in our waterproofs. When there were queues, we just waited in each other's embrace. We fed the ducks on Windermere as we ate ice creams and then we went to the quieter town of Buttermere and stayed in a hotel called *Fish Hotel*, which amused us. We were so happy just being together. It was always effortless, and such fun!

When we returned from the Lake District, Michael extended his stay for another two weeks - again without pay. I however, still had to go to work and so for a wonderful fortnight, we lived like a normal couple sharing a flat. I kissed him goodbye in the mornings and came home in the evenings to him cooking dinner, always upbeat. I'd never lived with a guy before, but it was like we'd had this routine forever.

He was so resourceful. He took it upon himself to drive my car to the shops and found all the independent delis and grocers that I'd never been able to afford to shop in. I came home to exotic cuisine that I'd never eaten before, prepared from fresh ingredients. King prawns in garlic oil or quinoa, which was seen as a middle-class delicacy then. He loved his wines and had brought over from Australia a vintage bottle from the 70s. Now was the time to finally drink it.

One day, I came home to him installing a shower hose in my bath! He'd gone out and bought one to attach to the tap, and a shower curtain. He couldn't believe that I didn't have one. 'No one in Australia has baths!' I remember him laughing. 'There's always time for a shower, but not always time for a bath.'

I was so impressed. He was so practical; so dynamic. This was another example of me challenging my life-long belief that we must accept things as they are. Just like the umbrella incident in the Turkish café, I never considered that I could take things into my own hands and upgrade my bath to a shower even though it was a rented property.

It was small things like this which symbolised an unlocking of my own true voice. Michael awakened me to freedom of choice. He asked me once, 'Why do you have short hair?' I didn't have an answer. I'd never questioned it. I'd always envied girls unpinning a ponytail and unleashing long, flowing hair, but I simply presumed that I didn't have that kind of hair, because my parents always kept mine in a bob.

I had not been the true, fully expressed version of myself until I met Michael. It was like he gave me a stage to be seen and heard. I felt appreciated for all my qualities – even the ones that hadn't fully blossomed yet. He enabled me to develop my wit too. I had his sense of humour, but it had always been suppressed so I'd never considered myself very funny. But with him, I was high vibe and discovered I could now engage people with much more confidence and make them laugh.

Ironically, despite him being my biological father, he left me feeling more like a woman and less like a child than anyone ever had. The disassociation from myself, which I always felt as a child, was dissipating. I was discovering my true nature, thanks to this man, and he was loving me.

Because Michael extended his stay, the short period of grace where I had my flat all to myself had ended and my flatmate, another physio colleague from the hospital, had moved in. Michael and I were openly sharing a room by now as I had long abandoned sleeping on the sofa. She knew he was my biological father, and she must have known what was going on, but she never gave me any signals that she thought this was inappropriate. Perhaps she assumed we were being considerate by not invading the shared living space.

One scene in our precious video shows her, my childhood friend Lisa, Michael and me giggling our heads off in our living room. Michael and I are seen clinking glasses through linked arms and being tactile. They must have seen the electricity between us. It was clear that our connection was far more intimate than you would expect between a long-lost father and daughter making up for lost time.

Whatever my flatmate thought, she couldn't have judged too harshly because the three of us enjoyed many lovely evenings cooking together. Years later, she invited me to her wedding, which regretfully I could not go to, and I often think about her.

Beneath the laughter though, there was an implicit acknowledgment that we were on borrowed time. Michael and I knew there was agony to come. We knew he had to go back to his life. We knew our love was forbidden. We knew we had no future.

In retrospect, this is where I expect pre-union counselling might have helped me to understand the intensity of feelings we were both experiencing, and recognise that I was in emotionally dangerous territory. It could have warned and protected me.

Possibly I would have been able to redirect my feelings, with support, into a more familial framework. But our love was so uplifting that we were washed along with the tide of it and less able, or willing, to deny it or reject it as each day went by.

Chapter 7

An Unexpected Guest

1990

When the inevitable day loomed for Michael to go back to his life and his career, we had spent six incredible weeks together. Every waking minute was magical and our love all-encompassing. I couldn't now imagine life without him.

After our tearful goodbye at the airport, I drove home solemnly but with a spark of hope in my heart. Somehow, I knew he'd find a way and we'd see each other again soon.

We spoke daily by phone. In my new apartment, we had a landline in the lounge, so no more payphones in the corridor. I had no idea what international calls cost and never thought to find out. But when my next phone bill arrived it was £800! I only earned £700 a month. When I told Michael, he transferred the money to pay for it. After that, we found some cheaper phone card deal.

Both of us were in turmoil about whether we should pursue this costly love we shared. We both knew we were on the edge of an unknown abyss that could consume both our lives.

I fluctuated between hope that we could somehow be together, and resignation that there were way too many complications. Just a month after he left, in the September, I opened myself up to the prospect of normal dating, settling on the notion that an ongoing relationship with my birth father was neither acceptable nor feasible. While out with my childhood friend Lisa, in a popular pub in Fulham, two guys asked us out.

My date was called Sean, a banker who was generous, funny and ticked all my boxes, including the one for chemistry. But my heart hadn't let go of Michael and seeing someone else felt like a betrayal. Sean was happy to take things slowly and gradually I allowed myself to open up. I tried to withdraw from Michael and to shut my feelings away somewhere deep within. Often I didn't answer his calls, even though it pained me to ignore the ringing when I knew it was him on the other end.

After a few weeks I met Sean's parents and we stayed overnight. I remember his mum bringing us breakfast in bed, so she obviously approved of me. I also remember staying over at Sean's house one night and getting locked in. One of his flatmates locked the door with a key from the outside, not knowing I was there. With no mobile phones, I had to shout out of the window and ask for someone's help to track down Sean at work!

They were happy times, made more so perhaps because it was such a contrast from the stressful secrecy surrounding my time with Michael. I couldn't deny I still loved him deeply and pined for him, though of course I tried to hide this. I missed our easy connection so much! I did confess to Lisa how I felt, but stopped short of telling her we had consummated our feelings. She quickly reminded me how inappropriate a relationship with him would be, and reminded me how great Sean was and that I'd be mad to throw him away for something so tumultuous, so forbidden.

Lisa's relationship with the guy she met on the same night that I met Sean was also going well and over Christmas, the four of us plotted a ski trip to France, driving there by car.

I told Michael I was going away for Christmas. By now he was getting anxious about my reduced calls. He understood why I was trying to withdraw, but it didn't make it easy to accept. His heart ached for me and he was torn between letting things take their natural course and making a stand to fight for our love. He asked who I was going with, and I causally replied, 'A friend and two guys.'

'Where are you going?' he asked.

'I don't really know the details. The others booked it. It's a place called Meribel.' I felt bad for being so cagey with him. I knew he could feel me slipping away, which upset him. It felt wrong to try to move on so soon, but I was in turmoil and wanted to remove myself from this stressful situation.

It was a happy car journey to Meribel, in the French alps, with us all singing songs on the car radio. But Michael was never far from my thoughts. On Christmas Eve, two days into our trip, I came off the slopes early, in need of a nap. There was a knock on the door, and I expected it to be Sean, returning from the mountain. But it was Lisa, with a wild look in her eyes.

'He's here, he's here!' She cried before I had chance to say anything.

'Who's here?' But as I uttered the words, I knew in my heart who she meant.

'At the ski lift, there was this photo…' she spluttered. 'It's of you!'

She handed a piece of paper to me. It was torn at the edge, from where she had ripped it off the metal post. On it was a photocopied photo of me. Underneath, written in marker pen, it read: 'Bon Noel! I am at Hotel Coucou,' and it gave the street name.

Neither of us could believe our eyes.

'What? Where was it? Who's seen it? Has Sean?' My mind was racing both at the prospect of Michael being here - the tenacity of trying to trace me; and then, what would Sean think?!

'No, I grabbed it before anyone else could see. I don't know how many of these there are though – there may be more.' Lisa replied.

It transpired that Hotel Coucou, which means Hotel Cuckoo, was just a stone's throw away from our chalet. I was burning to run over there and throw my arms around Michael. But I couldn't. As a duo of couples, I didn't want to disrupt the dynamic. We had a meal planned in two hours and tomorrow was Christmas Day.

I waited until Boxing Day before I did anything. But I was

distracted for the whole festive period. When I awoke on Christmas morning next to Sean, my mind went straight to thoughts of Michael. When I opened my Christmas gift from Sean, I was imagining what it would be like exchanging gifts with Michael, in bed together. I pictured him alone on the most emotive day of the year, wondering if I'd seen the photocopied sheets of paper dotted around the resort. Maybe he was out taping more copies to metal posts now! I couldn't believe he had come all this way, on his own, at Christmas to find me.

We had a real tree in our chalet room, which we decorated. We cut one down from outside and smuggled it inside. After breakfast we had Christmas lunch on the mountain in a gorgeous restaurant, then skied it all off in the afternoon. The whole time I thought about Michael, flitting between worrying about him being on his own, imagining the feeling of our first embrace and then fretting about bumping into him while with Sean. Every time we passed a ski lift, I tried to chat to distract Sean just in case there was a another one of those '*Bon Noelle*' photos of me!

On Boxing Day morning, I at last got my chance. The others went skiing and I said I wanted a chill day after too much Christmas champagne. I still hadn't outright told Lisa my secret, but she knew exactly what I was up to. The boys, on the other hand, blindly accepted my excuse and Sean kissed me fondly as he left for the slopes. I called Hotel Coucou from a phone box so as not to incur a charge on our room and gave Michael's name. I got through to him first time.

'I couldn't wait.' He explained. 'I needed to tell you how I feel – in person. I couldn't bear you just slipping away like this, when I know what you must be going through. Can you meet me at the café by the statue in the town square at 11.'

Fifteen minutes later, as I approached the cafe, I glimpsed him through the window. He looked tired and anxious. My heart swelled with love. I knew in that moment that there was no going back, no denying that this time we were going to pursue our flame of love however forbidden or misunderstood it may be.

We greeted each other with a tight tear-jerking embrace.

'I've been through endless days and sleepless nights of soul searching,' He relayed. 'And I resolved that this love we share is a love that has eluded me my whole life. And it's mutual! If I don't fight for it, I will always regret it. I needed to show you how committed I am to our love, whatever challenges may lie ahead.'

'And that's why you came?'

He nodded. Perhaps this was an expression of paternal love on some level, like a dad going to the nth degree to prove his love. Only, Michael hadn't been a dad, and our love unfolded like romantic love, not like fatherly love, and so he didn't know how to contain the actions – but the expression was the same.

'Even if we can't be together, I want you to know that I'll always love you. If nothing else, I hope that will help with your inner conflict.' He finished.

And that's why he flew from Australia, with no knowledge of my whereabouts, and bravely checked into a chalet hotel on Christmas Eve, intent on finding me somehow.

'I love you so much too.' I was crying now. 'Oh my god, what are we going to do?'

I felt deep compassion. I noticed how thin he looked and concluded it must be from the angst of the last few weeks, not helped by debilitating jetlag. No one had ever declared abiding love for me before and it felt sincere and life affirming. Working on a hospital ward, I had seen gritty sides to life; As a child, I'd moved from school to school; I'd had richer experiences than most, but I'd never felt anyone truly had my back. I knew Michael did, 100 per cent. All the memories of our happy, happy holiday came flooding back.

He told me that before he even went to bed after his 24-hour journey, he set out with several photocopies of his favourite picture of me, and taped them onto ski lift support posts and on the windows of après ski bars. The resort was bigger than he had expected and when he was satisfied that he'd covered the main access points to the slopes, he stood on his balcony, gently calling my name and praying to find me. He was tenacious and creative when he had to be. He had even carried the original photo around with him and asked English skiers if they might have seen or met me.

'I kept feeling this urge to look in the direction of your chalet, through the trees!' he said, and we laughed partly with relief and partly astonishment at our ethereal connection.

'I can't believe how close you were. I could practically wave to you from our balcony.' I laughed.

We hugged and cried, and cried some more, as it dawned on us that this precarious love affair was far from over. Then we went skiing. I knew I'd have to tell Sean and the others that Michael was here, but I didn't care what they thought now.

On the slopes, the pure white snow contrasting with the clear blue sky somehow felt symbolic of clarity for this fresh chapter. The landscape seemed to bathe all our frayed emotions of the last few months with a healing balm. I kept thinking how foolish I had been to try and deny what we had and how good and right it felt when we were together.

This feeling transcended everything. My worries and what I'd say to Sean paled into insignificance. I loved Michael and he was here, with me, and that was all that mattered! Our love felt like we could conquer all challenges, as long as we were together. I had tried to deny it, he had too. We were both conscientious, upstanding professionals who had never flouted the law or rebelled against social mores. All we wanted was to love each other – how could that be so wrong?

Back in the room, when the others returned from the slopes, I sat on the bed and told Sean that my dad had turned up.

'Your dad? How did he know you were here?'

'I think I told him I was coming here. He wanted to surprise me for Christmas. After all these years he's really keen to start a relationship.'

'But unannounced is a bit much isn't it?'

Sean knew I'd recently traced and met my birth parents. He

didn't know of my romantic feelings of course, but he sensed something odd about the whole thing, especially since Michael and I had spoken on the phone so much at the beginning of our courtship. For the remaining days of our trip, I tried to navigate giving time to both these men. For Sean though, he detected something had changed between us.

Then followed an awkward drive back to the UK with Sean and me in the back hardly speaking. We agreed to go to our own homes when we arrived back in west London, both saying something about needing sleep but knowing that there was now a distance between us - the reason for which I obviously felt unable to explain to him.

Within hours of me being dropped home, the doorbell rang and there Michael was, smiling on the doorstep. He stayed for another week. He was now in the process of setting up his own architecture practice – something he attributed to being in love because it finally gave him the energy required to spur him on to realise this entrepreneurial ambition. But it also meant that extending his stay further this time was out of the question.

In that one week, it soon became apparent that we couldn't live without each other, which meant that the only option was for me to move to Australia.

Chapter 8

Across The World

1991

Before making the big move to uproot my life to one of the furthest corners of the planet, we decided that I'd first go to visit for a month. This was more to satisfy my family, rather than to quell any doubts of my own. I could feel in my bones that my path would lead me to living with Michael on a more permanent basis. They of course did not know the truth. I let them believe I was taking a physiotherapy job and uprooting for an adventure, and the month-long visit was to check out the place.

The same can be said for my friends, though my two closest ones guessed the truth: Alice, since she had been by my side when I first picked up the phone to call my birth mother and then for the first airport meeting with Michael; And Lisa, who'd shared many fun evenings with Michael in my flat and saw my reaction to his arrival in our ski resort. Both have since told me that they thought the whole thing was odd, but they had the grace not to confront me outright. 'It was never for me to ask,' Lisa told me years later. She also reflected that she didn't really like what was happening, and felt back then that Michael, being an older man, should have had the intelligence to curb his feelings and not let our relationship develop so far. But she also liked him and saw that we were both happy.

Even if they had interfered, it would have been fruitless. Both were worried about me and loved me as their friend – I would have recognised that. But I also knew that they couldn't truly put themselves in my shoes because they weren't adopted. Throughout my life, I have always felt that no friend can wholly understood the dynamics of being an adopted child. Just as I surely wasn't privy to their own unique experiences.

I would have dismissed them as not understanding the depth of magnetism between us. In a lot of forbidden relationships, especially when an older man is involved, everyone thinks it's the male who should put the brakes on, but when there's mutual chemistry, all parties are equally responsible. When fervent attraction is involved, we are often helpless to control our feelings. As humans, we are oftentimes inappropriately attracted to people – yet we all judge each other for it.

In our case, we had an even more powerful force working against us – a known, but not well understood, psychological phenomenon which we were yet to be aware of; something which would strip anyone in our situation of the ability to swim against the tidal wave of their emotions.

And so, at the end of March 1991, I visited my forbidden love for a whole month. After a long and painful separation of two and a half months, it had felt like a lifetime.

Michael lived in a leafy suburb of Perth. I loved it instantly. It was autumn there and the days had a different quality about them. There were deep blue skies, and a warm balmy air, pregnant with the sweet smell of jasmine - intoxicating alongside the wonderful awareness of being with my soulmate. As Michael was building his own business, he took on freelance contracts for large architecture firms. It meant he sometimes travelled far and wide for a specific project and the firm would pay for his accommodation so that he could be on site for several days. I had nothing better to do so I went with him. I loved chatting on the long drives and playing our favourite music. Once, not long after I had arrived, we drove six hours through the night to beat the heat. I didn't mind because my body clock was all over the place anyway. It was enchanting to drive under the starry night sky, which looked different to the UK somehow. At two in the morning, it was still boiling hot.

I was quite happy spending an afternoon reading in a café or exploring the fascinating landscape around the town, which was so different to the UK. When he returned from his site visits, he'd tell me all about the projects. I was struck by how much of an intuitive and holistic professional he was. He looked beyond the technical drawings and the face-value job brief, asking his clients how they lived their lives. He would go to great lengths visualising them moving through their routines. On this particular project - a newbuild block of flats, he nudged all the bedroom windows by a few centimetres, so that every bedroom on one side of the building framed a full visual sunset. He recognised when one household would prefer impressive mod cons, and when another would prefer a more rustic set up. It was a display of his emotional intelligence at its height – at least that is how I saw it.

Back in his neighbourhood, on his days off, we went out sightseeing. 'Let's do that,' 'I'll drive us there,' 'You've got to see this,' he would enthuse, like anything was possible and nothing out of bounds.

I met some of his friends who knew I was his daughter. Michael couldn't hide that because before he came to visit me, he'd told them of his impending trip to England to meet his long-lost daughter and they were all excited for him. When he'd returned, they'd asked to see photos, so it wasn't an option to pretend that I was a girl he'd met while visiting London. Besides, lying just didn't come naturally to either of us.

One of these friends was the one I'd met in London before Michael visited – the one who commented that we drove in a similar way. We went for lunch and I remember us being tactile and free with each other. While we didn't kiss or hold hands, we clearly behaved and looked at each other like a couple in love. The friend must have picked up on it. But Michael didn't seem to care and neither did the friend.

I don't recall us ever making a definitive statement about it, but it soon became evident during my month-long visit that we loved each other beyond compare and found ourselves forming plans to be together.

'I'm going to get my practice up and thriving as soon as I can, become independent and support us both,' he vowed.

When I returned to the UK after my month-long recce, I started the visa application. I was impatient for it to be complete so I could leave the UK and start my new life with Michael as soon as possible. But in a serendipitous stroke of good timing, as I waited for the visa approval, I received a letter telling me I'd been shortlisted in a writing competition to win a place on a prestigious beauty therapy course.

I'd entered earlier in the year after spotting the words, 'Win A New Career' on the cover of a magazine. The prize was a Diploma in Beauty Therapy at a college in London. I'd always considered beauty therapy to compliment my physiotherapy and had even checked out courses from this very same establishment a few months earlier, only to find them too expensive.

To enter, I wrote a 500-word essay about being told I was adopted and becoming a physiotherapist because it was what my adoptive mum had done and then discovering my birth mother and how she had also followed a path to a similarly caring vocation through teaching and ended up working with special needs children. I tried to weave a story that was both poignant and inspiring.

Being shortlisted down to three got me an interview, and soon after that, I was told I had won! It was a big deal because there were 4,000 applications. The magazine which ran the competition did a big feature on me. There was a fancy awards ceremony in London, in which I needed to wear an evening dress. I dug one out, which had been creased in a cupboard. I clearly wasn't very domestic back then because running late, I thought it was a great idea to iron the neckline while I was wearing it. I burned my chest and went to the ceremony with a small but extremely sore red iron mark on my *decolletage*!

I immediately gave notice on my job in the rehabilitation unit at the hospital so I could start the three-month programme as soon as I could. I had to get the train and Tube to Bond Street every day from Monday to Friday. But I still needed to earn a living, so I took on night shifts on the reception desk for A&E at the same hospital. I happened to hear of a casual vacancy through a colleague and it was a case of being in the right place at the right time. Despite this being casual work, it equated to better pay hour-by-hour than my full-time professional physiotherapy role. I came home from the course on Friday evenings and went straight out to a night shift. Sometimes I did the Sunday night as well when I needed the extra money, and went straight up to the college on a Monday morning. I was exhausted.

Sitting at the gateway to the casualty wards, I saw all sorts – Friday night revellers coming in with alcohol poisoning, drunks who'd got into fights with fingers hanging off, car crashes, you name it. It was a formative life experience.

I was sleep-deprived and had no social life but it didn't matter because I was in love. All I was interested in was talking to Michael on the phone and getting the qualification under my belt ready for my exciting new future.

When my visa for Australia finally got approved, even though I was desperate to go and join Michael, I delayed my departure to finish the course. I had the foresight to know that when entering a new life in a new country, it would be prudent to have as many qualifications under my belt as possible to open as many doors as possible.

The training period was a happy three months. There were some gorgeous and extremely well-groomed girls on it and we all became good friends. It was summertime and in our lunch breaks, we'd sit in a park and eat our pre-made sandwiches. It turned out I had a natural talent for all the techniques. I sailed through the theory because of my anatomy and physiology training. I scored 90 percent and above in all my results. This was such a confidence boost for me, as I had never achieved these sorts of marks at school.

After I qualified, I was asked if I'd like to stay on as a tutor at the academy. If I wasn't about to move; if I hadn't met Michael, I would have said yes, and my career would have taken a different track. I'm a bit sorry not to have done that. But this was not meant to be and in August 1991, I set off for Australia on a one-way ticket.

Chapter 9

A New Life

1991

Michael greeted me at the airport. He had decorated his lovely home – *our* lovely home - with welcome banners and candles to celebrate my arrival, and a big note by the front door: 'Thanks for coming!'

There began our new life as a couple. Michael now had his own architecture practice up and running, specialising in designing high end residential properties or renovations. After his initial trip to England, when he met me for the first time, he had worked tirelessly to find his first few clients. His tenacity meant it wasn't long before he was able to secure the lease for a small office and advertise for a secretary. 'It was our love that gave me the energy to finally make this happen, after putting it off for so long.' He told me again when he showed me his tiny office proudly. That's what love does. It energises you!

In those early days he only had one or two projects on the go at any one time. When he couldn't find a suitable secretary, he suggested that I come on board as his practice manager. I did everything - scheduled projects in the diary, faxed over design drawings, sent invoices, answered questions on the phone – so I soon learned the lingo of design concepts, building envelopes and negative space. It meant we worked and lived together 24-7. The business was his pride and joy. He wanted to be known as the go-to creative architect who designed bespoke houses or extensions to suit people's lifestyles, not just aesthetics. He was on top of all the latest design trends, and sustainable technology even though it wasn't a common consideration back then.

It looked like I had everything I could wish for in our new life. I loved my job and learning about the intricate details of house design. At lunchtimes, we would close the office for an hour and go to one of the parks nearby for a picnic in the sun or go for a quick run.

Our small, leafy suburb of Perth was just as beautiful in winter as it had been in autumn when I left. (August is winter in Australia). Our small town was marked as an up-and-coming area for creatives, in contrast to the more traditional industries that Perth was known for, such as construction and manufacturing. My time there was right when there was an emergence of eclectic bars, restaurants and music venues. The people were laid back and outdoorsy. The climate was hot but not humid. Even the light was different to the light in England. It seemed to be clearer, sharper, sweeter. The sky was a different colour - a clear, baby blue. The air smelled fresher – alive with the scents of herbs and exotic flowers. It felt to me like my life had expanded and that I was expanding with it. '*Love is a many-splendored thing*,' goes the saying from the famous song with the same name. This is exactly what it felt like to me. It felt like the force of our love enabled me to grow; and at the same time made me feel at home and at peace.

Most of the time.

Bubbling under the surface was a constant ebb and flow of anxiety about the nature of our relationship. Was this wrong? Could we ever tell people the truth? If so, what would they think? If not, then how can we possibly live with a permanent secret?

On top of that, I was adapting to a different culture, away from my deeply rooted friendship groups. I felt different because of my accent. The most difficult thing was that many of Michael's friends knew I was his daughter so we couldn't act naturally in front of them. He still wanted to see these friends, but he couldn't be seen to bring his daughter everywhere with him - that would have looked weird. It had to appear like I was getting on with my own life in Perth – having moved here for an adventure, so when he went out to see these particular friends, I stayed at home alone.

These evenings always hammered home the impossibility of our situation. I remember sitting with a glass of wine, watching *Seinfeld*, aware of the tick-tock of the kitchen clock, and wondering what on earth the future held for us.

Once, he was invited to a dinner party where his ex would be. It was torture waiting for him to come back, alone with no new friends yet, imagining all sorts of scenarios. When he finally came back, in the early hours, I was drunk.

'You said you'd be home by 12!'

He wasn't used to being told off and didn't understand why I was so upset. There ensued our first ever row. The stress of our situation caused others like this. At the heart of each little bicker was the insecurity about our future.

This cautious dynamic should have extended to how we behaved when going out publicly together. We were clearly a loved-up couple. Just the way we looked at each other would make it obvious to onlookers that this was not a father-daughter type of relationship. Somehow though, Michael didn't seem as worried about us being seen together when out and about in the town. He just trusted that everything would be ok. This was a comfort to me and amazingly, we never did bump into anyone he knew while doing coupley things.

Over time though, he had to disconnect from the old friends who knew I was his daughter. It was not sustainable to keep me a secret. I don't know whether he consciously distanced himself or whether they just fizzled out. This must have been a grievance for him but if he was distressed about it, he never showed it. He was always fully present for me. Always upbeat.

The silver lining for both of us having lost touch with friends was that we were happiest *a deux*, in each other's company. We could always make our own fun. We experimented with cooking - he taught me so much in this department, using fresh herbs for new flavours and making things up regardless of recipes. Or, we dressed in silly outfits and danced in the living room to loud music. When we bored of that, we'd philosophise for hours.

Gradually we began to make new mutual friends, who didn't know our history. We didn't ever collaborate on a fabrication about how we met – that felt too contrived. But if we were ever asked, we said that we met when he was in England visiting his family. With him being originally from England, people probably assumed it was through mutual friends.

Aware that I needed to establish some independence, I took a part time job in a beauty salon and cut down my days in the architecture firm to three days. The beauty course, which I postponed my move for, did come in useful after all! Through this, I made some girlfriends. The salon was such a warm and friendly atmosphere that I befriended both colleagues and clients too. Female friendships have always been important to me – a value no doubt which emerged from boarding school which was when I first felt my true sense of belonging to a family. Perhaps that is why making friends comes easy to me. I'd find myself chatting to them and the next thing I knew, we'd be meeting in a park or a cafe for lunch.

Other friendships emerged through Michael's business. There was one couple in particular who Michael had designed an extension for. The lady would visit our office regularly to discuss the interior designs. She sometimes brought her two little girls, aged 4 and 6, and I would delight in playing with them. She quickly took a shine to me for this. We got chatting and immediately hit it off. I went round to their house for dinner a few times when Michael worked late and over time he got to know them too. Soon, we became close enough to this couple to tell them the truth.

It wasn't planned. We went to their house for dinner, and the conversation was flowing in such a natural way, that it just came out. I can't remember if it were me or Michael who said the words, but I only remember their reaction – one of pure acceptance and compassion.

'Bless you guys. What an ordeal to harbour such a secret. We are here for you and are honoured you have trusted us with this.' She said. There was not an inkling of judgement nor condemnation. We didn't tell them not to tell others. We didn't need to.

This female friend was several years older than me, and over the years became a close confidant, who supported me when I needed an ear. I'm still in touch with her today. Their acceptance gave me strength. The thing I had feared most was people's reactions to learning the truth, so when we were met with understanding, it gave us permission to express ourselves as a couple when out in public locally.

Even so, I still found myself regularly jolted back into our anxiety-inducing reality: There was constant friction between the sense of belonging and joy that goes with true love; and the sense of isolation, fear and guilt that goes with keeping a secret. When I allowed myself to ponder our future, the inner peace that I always felt with Michael by my side dissipated, and in its place, the icy fingers of fear would clutch at my heart.

Here I was, living in Perth, on the other side of the world from all that I had come to know, in love with a man I felt utterly safe with, but within a relationship that society would judge as taboo, and categorise as incest. The depth and joyfulness of the love we shared was completely incongruous with how it would be perceived by the outside world. This was the source of my constant turmoil.

We had long discussions about our predicament, deep into the night, under the moonlight in our delightful little garden. Time again, we questioned the dates that my birth mother had given about the pregnancy.

'Tell me again,' I said, 'How long were you seeing Janet before going to Australia?'

'Quite long, for me!' Michael replied, jovially at first before returning to the grave issue of timings. 'In those days, going with someone for six weeks was a long time. I met her at the beginning of summer, I think. When we first lay together, it was late summer.

The maximum we were together was six months. Maybe less. I think we only had sex around three times, at a guess.'

'And how many weeks was it before you went to Australia that she told you she was pregnant?' I kept returning to the details, even though clearly Michael's memory was patchy and his mind wandering to the nostalgic element.

'Two weeks, maybe three.'

'I was born in May, which means she must have got pregnant in August. You went to Australia in October, and you didn't see her in the weeks before you went. So that doesn't make sense.'

'I think I may have had a final fling with her just before. In my dad's study after we met at a party.'

'But for her to know she was pregnant, she would have had to have missed a period, so it doesn't add up.'

'But she was one of those girls who would just know on day one if she was pregnant!' Michael replied. It was pointless to linger on this timeline, which relied on twenty-five-year-old memories. But still, we let all manner of theories race through our desperate minds, as we grappled for a glimmer of hope that there had been some mistake. Maybe Janet lied, and she had slept with someone else? Michael was the son of a wealthy professor after all, so she may have thought it would benefit her to say that he was the father. Perhaps she thought that this respected family would have means to support her. There were no DNA tests in the '60s (DNA paternity tests were first used in 1988, after the process of DNA fingerprinting was first introduced in 1984). Making false paternity claims was not uncommon.

'I suppose that's plausible,' Michael continued to reflect on these theories. 'It was a very long time ago, and I didn't know her *that* well.'

It might sound weird to hear him reminisce about having sex with the person who gave birth to me. But I felt removed from it somehow. I understood that they were young, and their emotions around their first intimate experience were undeveloped. What we were actually talking about here was my own conception, but that went over my head. It's hard to explain and I don't expect people to understand it, because I don't really understand it myself. But Michael didn't feel like my father, so it was hard to identify with the baby being talked about as actually being me - strange as that may sound.

Anyway, these conversations gave us a basis for reasonable doubt over our biological relationship. Only a DNA test could confirm it but in 1991, they weren't anywhere near readily available to the general public. They also gave us the strength to broach the topic as to whether our relationship was comparable to incest. But in no way did it ever feel incestuous. I became more and more interested in the psychology of our dynamic. There was such polarisation between how right it felt, and how wrong society would deem it to be.

Chapter 10
Secrets Corrode
1992

In our professional lives, things were going swimmingly. Michael's architecture firm grew rapidly, and he was forced to work seven days a week for a while to meet project deadlines.

Seeing Michael's professional side was wonderful. He was courteous, warm and humorous with all his clients, as well as taking his skill incredibly seriously – a rare combination. He called them by their first names, which I was taken aback by at first. In all my jobs in my short professional life, this was not at all how we did things. I asked him why he addressed them so informally. He explained that we are all essentially equal, and if you use someone's first name, you relax them and it's much more conducive to a personable relationship. 'Only when I can read their personalities can I design their living environment.' He said. It's one of the big cultural differences between here and England, where people can be uptight about rank and file. Here, it's acceptable to treat people on the same level – to have respect but not put them on a pedestal.

If I'm honest, I sometimes felt a bit jealous when I heard him on first name terms with some female clients, laughing and joking at ease in his small consultation room. But when I saw how everyone warmed to him and what a welcoming environment he had nurtured, I soon came to the view that his approach was much better than the formality I'd been trained in. I really had no cause to be jealous as I trusted Michael implicitly. It was only a reflection of my own insecurities.

Michael delivered his suggestions on designs with grace, always making his clients feel it was their idea so as not to push back on them. For example, he told me that when he noticed one of this client's eyes light up when they talked about their garden, he decided to incorporate several indoor–outdoor spaces with lots of glass to create the feeling of outdoors, and he moved their kitchen sink so it faced a flowering tree! When another client mentioned they had aging parents, he politely asked if they might consider making the doors and stairway a little wider so that in the future it could be adapted for a wheelchair – something the client would never have thought about. It was no wonder that his client base quickly grew on word-of-mouth recommendations. The business which he had long dreamed of setting up was soon thriving.

When Michael was forced to work seven days a week, he employed his third architect so that we could take weekends off. This surpassed the limit to how many people could work from his tiny office so Michael decided the time was right to look for a bigger, more central location and see how big he could grow. He employed a salesperson too, with the ambition to become the most well-known collective of architects for high-end properties in western Australia. Knowing that his own office had to be his showroom, he started a relentless search for the perfect location which he could renovate himself, while still delivering on his current projects. He visited site after site when he was off duty. I was full of admiration for how much he could handle and maintain his cheery wit, charm and professionalism, and still have time for me.

And time he did make. On weekends we went anywhere we wanted to. We hiked and camped in the Jarrah Forests or the abundant John Forest National Park, just a few hours from us. Or we spent lazy days on the beach, reading to each other, body boarding and walking along the shore, skimming stones, collecting shells and me doing handstands and walking on my hands, much to the delight of any passing onlookers!

When winter came around, we flew to Melbourne, on the east coast, and went skiing - something we both loved and, thanks to my time in Sweden as a teenager, something I was good at. We enjoyed tennis and golf too. Though with golf, it was more about simply being on the beautiful golf course collecting lost balls and listening to the kookaburras chattering in the gum trees, than it was about the game. We shared the same love of outdoor sport and exploration of new places.

But beneath the surface of these golden days, our secret gnawed away. It wasn't just the fear of being exposed by our local community, I was troubled by the potential ripples from further afield. My parents, for example, thought I was living with friends. I had given them a PO box as an address. They wrote to me every week and it filled me with guilt every time I saw their handwriting, knowing that they couldn't even look up the name of the town where their daughter had moved to, on the other side of the world.

We had a second phone line installed in our house just for them to call. If that one rang, Michael knew not to answer it. My heart always beat out of my chest when it sounded, because it reminded me of the forbidden secret I was guarding. That ring tone became synonymous with lying – to the very people who had reared me.

After a year, I went back to England to visit them. It was lovely to connect to them and all that was familiar about England, but the three weeks apart from Michael was agony. I remember the hours and the pound coins I fed into phone boxes all over the place, as we told each other our news and longed to be together again.

Back in Australia, the weight of my conflict drove me to drink more alcohol than I had ever drunk before. I was now 26. Although I had been exposed to the darker side of life working in a casualty ward, and had travelled a lot compared to my peers, I still had a long way to go on my path to awakening, wisdom and conscious decision-making. I still didn't trust that it could be ok to break convention and choose this alternative path.

Michael however, had much more faith that things would be ok. He had 18 years more life experience than me. He had survived the challenges of moving away from his family as a teenager and adapting to a new country. This had equipped him to cope with anything with courage and a good heart. 'Everything will be ok, as long as we are together,' he would reassure me, and I'd feel soothed. For a while.

For our first Christmas Day together in 1992, we went to Bali. It was a much-needed rest after working so hard, and wonderful to be free to behave like a couple after the constant low-level risk of exposure back home. But it also reminded us that we couldn't spend our Christmases with family and friends. Could we ever? This reality – along with the residual stress of running his business – showed up as the occasional argument.

One night, for example, Michael was his excitable self and wanted to stay up late and I wanted to sleep. When he still hadn't come to bed at 2am, I got up and found him dancing on the balcony to music with a whiskey in hand. He was so happy, so carefree, so spontaneous.

This was his energy, which I loved, but I also envied it in some way. I hadn't had the upbringing that allowed that side of me to flourish yet.

'It's two in the morning, come to bed!' I snapped, judging him.

'Oh, you're so girls' dorm prefect,' He quipped, in reference to a story I'd told him about telling girls at my school to be quiet in the night. I took offence.

At that point in my life, I hadn't had another experience of an ongoing, healthy relationship. Michael was intelligent and I didn't feel that I was particularly. Sometimes I'd think, 'how can I be enough for him?' This is why I got jealous occasionally when I saw him talk and laugh with other women. Everyone found him so engaging. Perhaps I just didn't understand the freedom of this man. Often, he'd tell me to 'chill', which I also found infuriating. I wanted to be 'chilled', but I didn't have the maturity or self-confidence to be chilled like he was.

When we returned from our holiday, the anxiety continued to escalate and so did my drinking. It wasn't huge amounts, but more than what I'd ever been in the habit of before. When I met Michael, I hardly drank at all. For him, it was a part of his enjoyment of life and went with our pleasure of eating out. Australia has many 'bottle shops' to serve the outdoor BBQ and picnic culture. There was a popular, inexpensive sparkling wine called *Sea View Brut*, which became our go-to drink. We got into the habit of picking up a bottle on our way home several times a week and sitting on our rooftop or on the beach to chat and end the day. It became part of our routine and because I found the affects soothing to my inner turmoil, it became a go-to relaxation tool for me, which I wouldn't otherwise have been drawn to.

If I was ever tipsy or moody from the effects of it, Michael always managed me well. He never got angry with me. We went over and over the same ground about whether we had a future, whether we could ever be truly open about the origins of our relationship. What was so hard was that by nature, we are both very open people, and such secrecy was alien and uncomfortable to us.

It's important to relay that our relationship never felt weird to us. We felt an animal, biological drive to be with each other - drawn together like magnets. Like something inside had taken over us. It was intoxicating. Many people may blame Michael for letting our relationship progress as it did. They may consider him the predator. You may think, yes you can't help who you fall in love with, but why didn't he – the more mature one – put the brakes on before it got sexual?

But how was he supposed to relate to me as his child? He met me as a woman and saw me as a woman. It would be naïve to think that he could relate and talk to me like my dad when we met. I already had a dad. And a mum.

Michael had never been a father, so he hadn't exercised his paternal side. For years he lived with the guilt of giving up a child he conceived. For years, the curiosity of what happened to her followed him, growing like an untended weed in his mind. When he finally traced her, he wanted to give her the world. I felt that always. I know that Michael would have died for me on the spot.

When parents fall in love with their baby, they experience intense feelings. These of course don't manifest as romance because the dynamic is one of helpless child and responsible caregiver. But as I was now beginning to understand through the literature I'd read in the library, when parent and child meet in adulthood, the same intensity of the birth bond can bubble up, but because the care-giver dynamic doesn't exist, the bond can manifest as the only other type of intense passionate love we know, which is romantic love.

Words can't express the intensity of feelings and so those affected just want to fuse with each other. Sex opens the door to deep intimacy. It softens your cravings with warm, fluffy oxytocin, and that's why a sexual consummation happens.

Michael and I even caught ourselves fantasising about having a child together - the ultimate expression of love for each other. But then we would immediately check ourselves. Common knowledge was that if close biological relatives conceive, there could be genetic problems for the child. Michael explained it as like rolling a die. The DNA mix *could* cause issues, but not always. Besides, if being together was taboo enough, having our own family would bring impossible complications.

In the Australian spring of 1993, our conflict reached tipping point. I remember being at a friend's wedding. Beyond the glamour and the smiles and the touching best man's speech was the stark reminder that we could never have such a public celebration of our love.

'How can we carry this on?' I sobbed that evening when we were alone. My heart ached at the thought of us parting, but it was full of fear at the prospect of being discovered – by my family, by our friends, and worst of all by authorities. No matter which route I took, the outcome seemed to involve agony and drama.

Michael, as ever, was comforting in his reassurances that our love would see us through anything and all would be well. 'Five years or so, people will forget. We'll just keep going. It'll be ok.'

In all areas of our life, he was conscientious and capable and whenever he comforted me like this, I was able to push my fears away, trusting that he was right. But now, sadly, his reassurances were losing their efficacy. I just couldn't see a way ahead for us.

'What if my family want to visit?' I said in yet another soul-searching conversation days later. 'I can't pretend to be living on my own.'

There was no one particular thing that finally broke me, but rather a constant nudge towards the inevitable realisation that this couldn't continue. The fear of our unknown future and possible exposure tormented me more than I could bear. Though the words terrified me to utter, I concluded that I had to return to England.

We wept together night after night, but Michael never tried to change my mind. He was supportive of my decision to leave even though he truly believed we could make it. Although he was dying inside, he would not try and stop me.

Chapter 11
Wilful Lifeforce
1993

During the two weeks of preparation for my departure from our vibrant life here, to my old life in the UK, I felt utterly drained. It was a debilitating tiredness. I naturally put this down to the exhausting emotions of leaving. But it was Michael, ever prescient, who proposed there was something more at play. On the very day before I was due to leave, he handed me something that took me by surprise.

'I got this from town today. I think you should do it.'

I read the packet. It was a pregnancy test. A bolt shot through my stomach and according to Michael, I went white. I hadn't for a minute considered this. But now it seemed entirely plausible. I was speechless.

'Not here.' He continued, reading my face. Let's drive to the golf course and look at our view.' He was referring to one of our favourite spots where we often walked and looked for stray golf balls, collecting them in a bag like treasure. I packed a sample of pee in a little pot, and we set off in our old, beaten-up, open-top, white jaguar, in which we had had many happy adventures.

When we arrived at our viewing spot, I got out the pot and did the test. Those few minutes, staring at the little white circle on the test strip were interminable. I tried to focus on the beautiful view over an expansive lake, but I was drawn back to the plastic test strip. Slowly, from the white, a purple plus sign appeared. I felt my heart increase to a pound in my chest, as we both sat in shocked silence. I still have this test today, with the plus as clear as ever!

'Whatever you decide to do now, I'm behind you,' he said.

We returned home, about to spend our last evening together before our lives were shattered. Like robots, we went through the motions – the final packing and checking of flight details.

The thought of arriving back in England as its winter began, just as the Australian summer was beginning, alone, desolate and now, pregnant was a hollower feeling than I can ever describe. But it was too big to change tack so abruptly. We would just have to discuss what we were going to do over the telephone from the other side of the world.

I'd already told our friends and colleagues at Michael's practice that I was leaving. I don't think anyone viewed it as us splitting up. I said I missed home and that as an only child, I felt an obligation to see my parents more. I was still young and it would be clear to everyone that I was torn about moving my life and nationality for good.

The airport arrival the next morning was my darkest hour. Crying from the depths of my anguished heart, I tore myself away from Michael's embrace to walk through the departures hall. The look of love and despair on his face is forever etched in my mind.

I had company on the plane. After I'd booked, I discovered that the secretary at our practice was also on the same flight – excitedly travelling to the UK for the first time to visit distant family. Somehow, we managed to get seated together. At first, I was delighted to have companionship, but after yesterday's bombshell, it now felt like a hindrance not to be able to weep privately with the full force that this sorry situation called me to do.

She was under the impression I was going back just for a couple of months. I didn't want her to know too much because she worked with Michael and the other four colleagues in his office. Trying to maintain my composure, I answered her eager questions about where to go in England. It turned out to be a comfort to have some distraction from the inner pain. Until, halfway through the flight, I went to the toilet and to my horror, saw blood in the toilet basin.

'My baby, my baby, please, no, don't let this be a miscarriage,' I muttered aloud. Even though I had not come to any conclusions at that point about whether I was going ahead with this unplanned and complicated pregnancy, when I saw the decision slipping from my hands, it was a visceral reaction to try to protect this life inside me.

I composed myself enough to return to my seat, but it was now impossible to continue the small talk and I had to pretend to be asleep. I really don't know how I kept things together. It was the longest journey imaginable.

When we eventually landed on British soil, the tears were rolling down my cheeks. Exhausted, emotional, bloody and cold just looking at the damp, dull autumnal weather out of the window, I collected everything I now owned in the world - crammed into two suitcases - from the luggage belt and went straight to A&E.

I waited a couple of hours to be seen and had a scan. To my utter relief, I was told everything was ok. When I was eventually discharged, now mid-morning, I'd been awake for almost 48 hours. I headed to Lisa's house in a taxi. She'd moved in with the same guy from that fateful ski trip, but sadly their relationship had run its course and now she was in that awkward phase of living with an ex while she figured out where she was going to move to.

She was excited that I was coming back and we could flat hunt together in Clapham. She thought we'd be two single girls having a ball. When she suggested drinks on my first night back, I had to tell her I was pregnant. I could detect her disappointment, along with shock, on her face.

'By who?!'

'A guy I dated - he wasn't really a thing. His name is Grant,' I'd already gone through my alibi but I wasn't used to lying, especially to my dear friend whom I'd shared everything openly with since I was 11. It pained me to lie to her.

She was very supportive, but it was clear that this changed things for her. I remember her saying, eyes wide, 'What are you going to do?' and me sighing, 'I don't know!'

Day by day my belly swelled, and I still had no answer to that question. I was acutely aware that I was now grappling with the same dilemma experienced by my own mother years earlier. My heart went out to her as I imagined her as a teenager, with less options and less freedom to talk to understanding friends. The irony wasn't lost on me that she too had been carrying Michael's child. It crossed my mind that I could consider adoption. But there was no way I could repeat the family pattern, bestowing onto another life the separation and subsequent soul-searching that had overshadowed my own.

Lisa stood by her promise that we would live together despite the change of circumstances. One afternoon, while we were being shown a flat by an estate agent, I started to feel strange. I asked to use the bathroom and to my horror found that again, I was bleeding. This time it was heavy. Huge clots were falling into the basin and splashed up the side. It was all over my jeans. There was so much blood, this *must* be a miscarriage.

'Sorry, I don't feel well. We have to go,' I gasped when I emerged.

Lisa could tell by my face something was very wrong. Then she saw the blood on my clothes. She hailed a cab and we went straight to the Chelsea and Westminster A&E. I was taken to the gynaecology unit immediately. They did a scan and then, 'bum-bum bum-bum'. The sound of a heartbeat, loud and clear. I was presented with an image of the foetus on a screen, moving rhythmically.

'This is clearly a strong one.' The clinician reported. 'Everything is fine, but I'd recommend you rest and check in with your GP for regular checkups.'

In that moment, everything changed for me. When I saw that little being inside me, an overwhelming feeling of attachment and urge to protect kicked in. I didn't want to lose this baby, no matter what. It was our baby, conceived in love. It was all that I had with me now of Michael.

The medics didn't know why I was bleeding, but that didn't

matter. I had not miscarried and my decision had been made for me. The scan was held up to me, showing the little life inside me; I heard its heart beating. I just knew that this was meant to be.

Chapter 12

Love Will Find a Way

1993

Soon after that, Lisa and I found a flat to rent in bustling Hammersmith. I got a job as an assistant physio at a sports clinic. The contrast between my beautiful sunny home in Perth with the man I loved, who made me laugh every day, and this pokey flat on a noisy, London street and a crowded daily Tube commute was unbearable. My life lost its joy and meaning. The only thing that kept me going was the life growing inside my tummy and wanting to stay strong to give them the best start in life.

Cue yet more long-distance phone calls and agonising over what to do. I had left Australia because of the fear of being found out, but it seemed that no sooner had I made the decision to leave, that events had conspired to make me reconsider. We were already finding our separation intolerable, but now that I knew our baby was here to stay, it made us want to fight again for a way to be together.

Years later, Lisa recalled that during this time, I was sad and stressed and very far from the joyful, open and fun person she knew. Sometimes we fell out. It was hardly surprising. I was consumed by my dilemma. She was still reeling from a breakup, had started a new job and now, she was contending with the fact that instead of living with her partying partner-in-crime, as she'd imagined, she'd be living with a hormonal, pregnant mother-to-be; and then a newborn! The phone was constantly ringing with Michael's voice on the other end, proclaiming how much he was missing me with his whole soul. This frustrated Lisa who would roll her eyes and say, 'It's Michael again!' How she never confronted me about what must have been a very obvious lie, I do not know!

I told Lisa and my parents that I had got pregnant by the fictional 'Grant', who I had been casually dating in Australia. My parents were not happy either. They encouraged me to have a termination, telling me that being a single mum would ruin my life. I was horrified at this suggestion. But how could I possibly tell them the truth? Oh, what a complex web we weave!

Their suggestion was particularly offensive to me because it triggered existential questions about my own fate. How different things would be if my own birth mother had been made to have a termination. So different that I would not have the chance to even deliberate this dilemma! This made me appreciate even more how precious and miraculous life is, regardless of the circumstances surrounding our birth into this world and how grateful I was to be alive.

Since that first heartfelt prayer, aged 17, while working as a live-in nanny, I had vacillated a lot on the topic of whether there is a God. Initially that experience gave me faith in the Church, and it prompted me to pray and attend bible study classes. But my years working in a hospital, witnessing suffering, indiscriminate injuries and illnesses had made me question it. What sort of 'God' would allow such human pain? Also, when I had shared my Christian beliefs with friends or colleagues, I had mostly encountered resistance to it. So, I found myself thinking, what reason is there to believe in God's existence, when most people around me didn't.

I gradually drifted away from the Church and the stories of the bible. I had long stopped praying and reconciled that life is just a series of random events, over which we have little or no control. But now, faced with the realisation that my mother could very well have chosen to terminate me, I returned to the belief that I was meant to be here; providence had seen to that. Perhaps there was some divine force that guides us through life after all, whether we're aware of it or not.

Since then, I have been drawn to many books by spiritual masters, which have informed my beliefs and given me insights into the inner urging of every human soul to remember their true nature. Some examples are *Conversations with God* by Neale Donald Walsh, *The Power Of Now* by Eckhart Tolle, *Autobiography of a Yogi* by Paramahansa Yogananda, *In Tune With The Infinite* by Ralph Waldo Emerson and *The Power of Intention* by Dr Wayne Dyer.

Through these, I have begun to understand that when I uttered that prayer all those years ago, and experienced that strong connection to something mystical, I was tapping into a divine power, which is not necessarily the 'God' that Christianity refers to. Rather, it is a power that I now believe orchestrates perfection in the universe, to which we are all connected – an all-loving, infinitely-organising intelligence which is both a creator and a presence within all life. The anthropomorphic interpretation of 'God', presented to us under many religions, which sees us born as sinners, needing forgiveness, instils fear and division. Whereas the spiritual teachings I came across in later years pointed to a universal 'oneness' and an inherent connection to divine love.

The works I read led me to understand that spirituality goes beyond religiosity. We all tread our own unique path, which leads us to where we're meant to be. If we earnestly seek to connect with our true divine nature, we will be guided there. All roads lead to 'God' no matter what terminology you choose. I refer to it as 'prime creator' or 'source energy' – a force which permeates and orchestrates the whole of creation.

At the tender age of 17, when questions about our existence were beginning to arise, I was searching for answers outside of myself. I had no idea then, that the answers were hidden within the chalice of my own heart, and that all I needed to know would be revealed if I tuned in to the guidance of my higher self.

Unfortunately, I didn't have that level of awareness when I was pregnant. It just felt clear that I should have faith and let life take its course. The near miscarriage reminded me that we're not the ones who give life. A baby grows inside us, but we don't have control over the life force that sustains it, just as we don't have control over the life force that birthed us, beats our hearts and moves the breath of life through our lungs.

As the weeks went by, the miracle of this living seed growing within me, into a fully functioning human being, felt more and more profound. Never having had any connection to a biological relative made it ever more powerful - like a taste of completeness. I cannot count the times I returned to the thought of the pain my birth mother must have gone through when she was forced to part with me.

The prospect of returning to Australia carried the same dilemmas and fears as when I left. But the idea of staying in London and giving birth on my own felt even worse. Eventually, I made the huge decision to return.

As soon as I did, a calmness settled over me. I bled on and off for the first three months of my pregnancy, but still, the baby hung on in there. We were really going to do this - there was no turning back now. Michael and I loved each other and now we loved our unborn child together. We knew that somehow love would find a way.

Chapter 13

A Mother's Wound

1994

I was six months pregnant by the time I flew back to be reunited with Michael in the January of 1994. Departing at the beginning of a new year felt propitious for a second beginning

As I prepared for my return, I felt the burden of indecision lift. Turmoil gave way to hope. I shipped all my belongings over in boxes, which Michael kindly paid for. Lisa accompanied me to the airport and as we were queuing for check-in, I had a surprise guest. My mum turned up!

We weren't on great terms since she'd tried to steer me to end my pregnancy and we had had an awkward Christmas together. Of course, she was saying this for my own good because, to her knowledge, I had no one to support me. Her unexpected appearance was an offering of an olive branch but I was so shocked to see her, I fear I may not have given her the warm and forgiving greeting that she hoped for. When I look back, I feel nothing but compassion for her. She could never have understood the complex layers of emotions I was experiencing because of the parallels between my current situation and my birth mother's story. It was so sensitive for her, she preferred to leave well alone so there was no way I could share with her what I was going through.

Soon, the loneliness and drabness of my life in a small London flat was replaced by the joy and fulfilment of being back with Michael. I was now 29 and he was 48. He looked after me in the best possible ways. We found out the gender of our impending arrival – a boy! After much deliberation we decided we would call him James, which derives from the Hebrew name Jacob and means 'May God protect'.

We talked and sang to him in my tummy, using his name and telling him we couldn't wait to meet him. I went back to work in the beauty salon part-time and continued to do some admin work at Michael's office to fill in the gaps. For all intents and purposes, we were known as a happy couple expecting our first child.

It was the height of summer in Perth when I arrived and one of the first things we did was organise a camping trip. I was getting larger by the day and Michael didn't let me carry a thing despite us having tents and stoves and all sorts of kit! I loved the freedom that being out in nature offers. I remember going to a BBQ of the friends whose wedding had evoked all those strong emotions just before I left for England. In sharp contrast to that, I remember laughing a lot, feeling the pregnancy hormones filling me with happiness and a warm nesting instinct.

Occasionally though, the enormity of our situation would again haunt me. Anxiety would clutch at my insides at the prospect of bringing a child into this completely unknown territory. But I would push it away. Predominantly, I was in a happy place, looking forward to the birth of our little boy – who was conceived in love and would be surrounded by love.

I sometimes fretted that there might be something wrong with our baby given our biological relationship, but Michael had no such concerns and assured me that all would be well. He told me about a dream he had one night of a little boy, about six months old, standing up in his cot with big blue eyes and blonde hair and for some reason I knew this was a very positive sign.

We gathered all the paraphernalia that one needs when there's an infant on the way, and spent hours painting free-style art on the nursery walls. Michael's artistic talents still fill me with awe. He decorated James's new room in bold, colourful, wiggly lines, all synchronized, with *Paddington Bear* murals blended in. It had a whacky psychedelic feel to it and I loved it.

We eagerly awaited the big day, though it wasn't without some sad moments as we dearly wished that we could share the excitement with our family and friends in the UK. Michael had a younger brother and sister and neither they, nor his parents, knew of our relationship. They were under the impression that I had gone to live in Australia to spend time with him and experience a new country. As outgoing, gregarious people, it felt an unusual position to be totally reliant on each other for love and companionship. That was the price we paid for our forbidden alliance – but one that we willingly accepted in order to be together.

I awoke one morning in April, two weeks ahead of my due date, with contractions and my waters broke. Michael immediately slipped into his calm, reassuring advisor mode. He had read up all about labour and told me we didn't need to go into hospital until the contractions got more frequent and stronger, so I tried to relax in the garden. But wow, the pain of contractions was like nothing I had ever experienced. It was scary because I didn't know what a normal level of pain was, or what was yet to come. We had booked into a small, private, maternity hospital not far from our home where we would have our own room and lounge area. We arrived there that afternoon as the contractions became more painful and I was told that I was well on my way to giving birth.

We'd decorated the room in advance with our personal markers to make it homely. We set out candles and photos and most poignantly, a poster which we brought back from Turkey of an azure sky; fuchsia flowers, which we had seen everywhere on our holiday; a rustic stone building in the foreground; and the word, 'Turkey' on the bottom. It represented all the aspects of the precious beginnings of our relationship.

There was a stereo and Michael even remembered to bring a tape with a compilation of our favourite Turkish music. Because the lyrics were foreign, we didn't attach to the words, so it provided simple, soothing, exotic sounds.

Not that I was paying much attention to the music now. Pain gripped my whole body like an iron pressure. These days, new mothers preparing for birth are taught breath work, and it's all about believing in the power and intelligence of the body to do what it needs to do. But there were no holistic approaches like that back then, not that I knew of anyway! I had no concept that my body could, and would, open up nicely if I just stayed present and breathed through it. Instead, I was anxious and obsessive over how on earth something so big could come through this tiny hole.

'It's so painful. Oh my God, it's so painful!' I cried.

A nurse attached a tens machine to my back, but it didn't help. It is supposed to distract from the pain of contractions by delivering low voltage electric impulses to the skin, but because I wasn't mindful, nor breathing consciously through it, as I now know to do, it was just bloody annoying to have electrical shocks as well!

By late evening I was having what's known as double-peaked contractions, which feel like a single contraction with two peaks. Suffice to say they were agony. I reluctantly agreed to a dose of a strong opioid-based pain killer called pethidine. I'd learned about this in my physiotherapy training and I knew you needed two nurses to sign to take it out of the controlled drugs cupboard due to its strength. I had been resisting this drug because I was thinking my baby would get a dose of it too, but I was so contracted, tense and anxious now, that I would have agreed to anything. I soon regretted it though because I still felt the pain and it made me feel woozy to boot! I vomited repeatedly in the shower in the corner of the hospital room.

The day staff now handed over to the night staff just as things were heating up. I didn't know how I was ever going to push this baby out of me. It seemed impossible that something so big could come out of such a small opening without splitting me in two!

The midwife assigned to me for the night had the same name as my adoptive mum, which I found to be an interesting synchronicity. She was calm and with our music playing gently and the candles flickering softly, I felt in safe hands. Michael filmed the whole thing on his beloved camcorder, positioning it on a tripod at the end my bed. At around 2am, baby James arrived safely into the world, two weeks premature. He weighed a healthy 6lbs 7ozs.

Spaced out from the pethidine and the exertion of pushing, I looked on wide-eyed and anxious as the midwife checked him over. My eyes sought out Michael's for reassurance and for a moment, time seemed to stand still.

'Is he alright?' I could hardly contain myself.

'He's perfect.' she smiled and laid him gently in my arms.

I cannot describe the relief I felt. Leading up to the birth, I hadn't explicitly expressed concerns about the risk of genetic mutation, abnormalities or birth defects that might result from us being first degree relatives. But I would be lying if I said I didn't have any. Michael had taken it upon himself to research genetics and heritage and had told me that when close relatives conceive, there's a higher risk of health problems or gene defects because the child has a higher chance of receiving a double dose of a recessive gene that may cause problems. It's not a guarantee of harm but it's a gamble.

For me, as a first-time mother, I would have done my fair share of fretting about my baby's health, regardless of who the father was. I could hardly believe an intricate, fully functioning perfect human being could possibly come out of me!

Michael took a photo - one that I still have to this day - of me staring doe-eyed at James as he gazed calmly up at me with watery, blue eyes. 'Aren't you going to give him a kiss?' he said with his usual gentle humour, which roused me from my reverie, and I kissed my son gently on the forehead.

It was the most astonishing and beautiful experience of my life to hold this tiny, living being in my arms, knowing we had somehow created him. He carried on looking at me, like a wise old man. It was 2.30am when I put our new little family member to my breast for his first feed and we dozed together in and out of light sleep for the remainder of the night.

When my eyes opened in the morning, they immediately and instinctually searched him out and I was again struck with empathy for what my birth mother must have gone through. The unfathomable grief she must have felt immediately after my birth, her breasts swollen with milk, ready to feed her newborn, only to have me taken from her by a stranger in a white coat, to 'minimize maternal bonding', as she was told.

My relationship with James started long before his birth. He was part of the fabric of my being for nine months. As I imagined giving him away to someone else, it became clear to me in that moment that he would absolutely be aware of this separation. We were physically, emotionally, physiologically and spiritually connected and I knew that James would have been traumatised if I had simply disappeared from his life, like my young mother had to disappear from mine all those years ago.

Whilst pregnant, I read a book called *The Primal Wound* by Nancy Verrier, a psychotherapist and adoptive mother. She elaborates on what she calls a 'primal wound' - the aftermath of a child being separated from their mother. She coined this phrase after examining the different life-long consequences for adoptees, from early years through to old age.

Reading it had been a light bulb moment. It validated some of my recurring feelings – my mysterious sense of abandonment and loss, even though I was loved and accepted by my adoptive family. As I held my own baby, experiencing pure love in every fibre of my being, her explanation made even more sense. To be separated from him would have been unbearable.

It is common for people to think, 'What can a tiny baby know or remember if it's loved and cared for?' Verrier herself was of this mindset when she adopted her daughter, but she soon read the signs indicating that babies experience much more complex emotions than previously supposed.

Her book prompted me to read more widely about 'attachment theory', first proposed in the 1950s by the child developmental psychologist John Bowlby. He observed that children who were separated from their caregivers - even when given all their basic needs like food and shelter - suffered emotionally and developmentally. His decades of research led him to conclude that attachment is not a luxury, but a biological, psychological, and emotional survival system. It's an inbuilt mechanism, ensuring babies monitor the emotional warmth and predictability of their caregivers.

His theory is now the most widely accepted framework to explain how individuals form close relationships. The early bond with a parent provides a secure base for a baby – a sanctuary from where they feel safe to explore the outer world. When this bond is steady, the infant internalises self-worth, trust, emotional regulation and safety. When it is fractured by early separation - as often happens in adoption - it leaves behind what Bowlby called 'attachment trauma', the legacy of which is complex.

Without a tether to secure trust, the child's developing brain and nervous system become familiar with feelings of insecurity, longing and impulsivity – these thought patterns become their norm.

In adulthood, without strong self-awareness or therapy, some people who experienced 'attachment trauma' can continue to feel a heightened hunger for belonging. Their doubts about self-worth, sown from early separation, remain even when healthy connections are achieved later in life.

This can manifest as investing too quickly or intensely in anyone who offers warmth or affection, or difficulties setting boundaries for fear of rejection. The need to be loved can become so acute that it overrides discernment, leaving them open to unhealthy relationships simply because someone *feels* emotionally available.

Reading all this made me realise I had a lot of soul-searching to do if I was to fully understand and heal myself. And why, perhaps, I was here now, in love with my biological father, who was now the father of my child.

***

Michael stayed in the hospital room with me that night whilst James slept peacefully on my chest. The next morning, we bathed our son for the first time, which is also captured on video. Now I know that you don't need to bath a new baby, especially if they arrive early. Babies are born covered in a white, waxy substance called vernix. It covers their skin in the womb, acting as a natural moisturizer, and is full of good bacteria protecting against infection. The more premature they are, the thicker it is - like yoghurt in some cases. Conversely, if they are delivered late, the vernix starts to dry out and goes flaky on the newborn's skin. Babies aren't 'dirty' or course, and if I'd known what I know now, I would have left him as he was, to acclimatise naturally to life outside the womb. In our video, James looks like a little alien covered in this goo, which is actually one of nature's protective wonders. Perhaps this is why he did not at all enjoy being immersed in lukewarm water the day after he was born!

We marvelled again at how beautiful and perfect he was. When we left the hospital, giddy with the post-natal cocktail of oxytocin and endorphins, there was no sign of the strife surrounding our love. We felt and looked like any other pair of proud parents going home to begin our new life as a family of three.

Strapping James into the car seat underlined how tiny he was. Suddenly the vehicle seemed big and dangerous. My protective instincts were in full swing. It was a wonderful moment walking into our house with him, but bitter-sweet. There was a notable absence of extended family members cooing over our new arrival, or proud grandparents to introduce our son to. It was just the three of us.

The first few days and nights felt daunting because of his fragility. I was acutely aware how dependent on us he was for his very survival. I watched on endlessly as he slept, following the rise and fall of his miniature chest as he breathed, and hoped I was doing all the right things.

He and I took to breast feeding seamlessly and he soon proved to be a calm and easy baby. It didn't take me long to get my confidence and settle into a routine and Michael was wonderful with us both.

'We've done it!' I triumphed to Michael one day because that's how I felt. Our son, the product of our love was here, and we were loving every moment of life. He had big blue eyes and blonde hair, just like the vision in Michael's dream! When he looked into our eyes there seemed to be a wisdom - a knowing that was almost uncanny. Perhaps like any new mother in love with her newborn, I became convinced that these little eyes housed a special soul and that he shone brighter than other babies.

When James turned five weeks old, I was consumed by the thought that this was the age when I was taken from my birth mother and placed in the arms of another mother, to start a new life in Yorkshire. I had no doubt whatsoever that James was intrinsically connected to me as his mother, and that there was already a deep biological and emotional bond between us. We were a perfect fit, in complete harmony. If he had been taken from me and given to another female, looking into her eyes, smelling her smell, hearing her voice, even as young as he was, he would have known, felt and intuited with his whole being that something was wrong. What impact did that separation from my own mother have on my life and my subsequent perception of my worthiness to be loved? I found myself pondering this more consciously than ever before. A great sadness washed over me for the little baby who had been denied the most natural, primordial relationship of all – the one with her own mother.

I am so appreciative for all that my adoptive parents have done for me in my life, and I truly love them. They desperately wanted to be parents, and they were over the moon to have me to call their own. I don't intend my words to dishonour that relationship. They were a normal young couple, saddened by their inability to conceive, who chose adoption as a solution. They wanted to give love to a child, and at the time they were told categorically, by the professionals involved, that I was now their baby. Go away, forget about the birth mother and get on with being a family. There was no suggestion that their baby may be traumatised or that the birth mother would bear any pain for her loss.

I do not cast doubt on my parents' intentions. They were doing their best, and undoubtedly had my best interests at heart. What I want to convey is that I now understand that there is a recognised wound when a baby is relinquished from its mother - regardless of the love and care it receives from its new caregivers. Nothing can wholly take the place of the maternal bond. I believe that is why so many adopted people are driven to seek out their natural mothers and fathers, even when they have had happy lives with their adoptive family.

Chapter 14

Fear Returns

1994

I was resolute on being the best mother I could possibly be. I breastfed James exclusively and all the community midwife reports were glowing. I instinctively knew what he needed and when. Our bond seemed to grow deeper and more profound every day. I became truly enlightened on the sacred union that exists between mother and child.

But with this came a sadness for the baby that was me 29 years earlier, who had never been able to express that deep loss from separation. James was a gift, and as I loved and nurtured him, I felt I was also somehow loving my own inner child. I know now that this marked the beginning of a long, often painful, healing journey to love and accept myself fully just as I am.

As a family, we enjoyed every magical moment of being together and resolved to carry on our active, outdoor lifestyles. James spent much of his first six months on this planet in the fruits of nature. Despite being born at the beginning of the southern hemisphere's winter, we still went on adventures exploring the many varied terrains of splendour and beauty which Australia offers. We camped when the weather was mild enough, or went on long bush walks with James on my back in a steel-framed backpack in a tiny helmet. We even went skiing with him secured in the backpack as he giggled with delight.

I took him swimming regularly too - something I'd done a lot of whilst pregnant with him. Our shared love of the great outdoors was one of our greatest joys and we were adamant that we would not let having a baby make us any less resilient. We wanted nature to be as much as a teacher to James as it was to us.

Michael took to having a baby around seamlessly and this helped to instil confidence in me as a can-do mum. I was breast-feeding, so we never had to think about all the paraphernalia that goes with formula-feeding. We simply went into the hills, forest or to the beach knowing I could feed him as and when needed, with mother nature's perfectly tailored nectar on tap. Breastfeeding meant I knew when he got his first two teeth at five months old, because he accidentally bit me! I yelped at the pain. He never bit me again and I carried on feeding this way until he was 15 months old.

When the signs of spring arrived, we took him to the seaside for his first paddle in the cool waters of Cottesloe Beach. Michael and I enjoyed reading aloud to each other a lot, and that day we finished the book, *Catcher In The Rye* by J D Salinger, which deals with complex issues of identity, belonging, loss, connection and alienation. I found it a very memorable read as it encapsulated some of the weighted questions about my identity, belonging and life-path, which had recently begun stirring in me.

We were a happy, blessed unit. Except, that is, for the dark cloud that forever hung over us. The painful awareness that our relationship was considered wrong never went away. We felt and looked like a normal family and yet we were far from that.

Because of this, I could never feel completely carefree. I also felt sadness that I had no family or old friends from England to share my joy of motherhood. Even though this joy was impinged upon daily by my concerns for the future and how we would manage our secret as the years went by.

I joined a mother and baby group and made some lovely friends there, but the awareness that I held a secret from them caused me much stress. I kept thinking, 'Just imagine if they knew!' I am an open and honest person and so this pressure to keep something under wraps, coupled with the unpredictability about our future was a double-strength cocktail for anxiety.

When James was three months old, I found the courage to confide in another close friend. I had met her through the mother and baby group. By then, the only people who knew our secret were the couple from Michael's business connections, who we told over dinner in my early days in Perth. This time it didn't spill out, but was planned. I was nervous before telling her though. A lot was at stake because if she reacted negatively, she may distance herself or worse, tell the other mums. But I was moved to tears by her reaction. She embraced me with love and compassion for what I was navigating. In fact, she chastised me for not sharing sooner and told me she understood completely how this could happen and that Michael and I shouldn't be judging ourselves so harshly.

The relief to be able to talk about it was immense. Given how much I value friendship, it was a great comfort to know I had support from friends who were comparatively new to the long-standing friendships I had left behind in England. It gave me a glimmer of hope that we could share our secret with others as time went by, and that we might not be condemned in the way that we had feared.

By now, Michael had found the ideal premises to open his big-dream office to impress clients. The site was an old video rental shop in a central city location. It was a huge space spread across one floor, with the potential for a striking open-plan design. As a design-based service, the interior aesthetics, mood and layout were very important.

He took the shell of the building and got busy designing every detail of its renovation. He project-managed everything, right down to the carpentry for the bespoke furniture. He did all this while maintaining his current projects in the old office, and remaining a loving partner to me and a fully present dad for James.

He even found the time to sand and paint the wood for the beautiful reception desk and build some stylish tables for the waiting room. They were so eye-catching that later, when the office opened, many clients asked where they could buy them from!

Ever since James came along, Michael had vowed that he would do all in his power to ensure our happiness and security. I recall in the days after we brought James home from the hospital, him saying with a look of earnest, 'My life is dedicated to you and James now.'

Yet still, the seeds of doubt and fear kept springing up to sour our perfect garden of life. Always in the back of my mind was the fear that people would eventually learn the truth and judge us harshly. Even though I'd now told two sets of friends, and they had been understanding, I worried that others may not react quite so sympathetically. Fear of their reactions, and fear of losing friendships pervaded my whole psyche. And what about my parents? How could I hide this forever? What on earth would I do if they ever wanted to visit me here?

Having been adopted, I had always wanted so much to one day have a family - to truly belong with flesh and blood of my own, and to feel at peace. But instead, I found myself in a situation haunted by the same themes of separation, loss, regret and pain that had surrounded my own birth. Was this an inevitable pattern set by my own trauma?

The familiar anxious thought patterns took hold, and the underlying tensions came out in the occasional argument. Michael was always resolute that everything would be ok and didn't fret like I did, though he always understood my fears fully. How I wished I could be as confident in our fate as he was. We spent many evenings discussing what the right thing was, not for us, but for our son.

The tension built and when James was just six months old, I painstakingly concluded that there was no future here with Michael, living in secret, and that I should return to England once again. There, at least, I could bring up James without constant fear wearing me down about the dire consequences we could face.

Again, we found ourselves painfully processing my devastating decision, preparing to say goodbye, searching flights and packing on autopilot. Like fugitives on the run, we would always be uprooting and making huge sacrifices for our love.

Michael was not only losing me this time, but also his beloved James, who he had devoted his life to. Looking back, I often wonder how I found the strength to leave the warmth and support of this man, who meant everything to me. Or indeed how I could take James from his devoted daddy, knowing what I know now about bonding and attachment. I can only draw the conclusion that my need to find relief from the searing anxiety that was my daily companion overrode everything. The fear of being condemned for our relationship was even greater than the unbearable thought of being apart from Michael. My thought process was that if I distanced myself from our relationship, I could embrace a normal life, free from fear. We would be safe. Our secret would be safe. It wasn't just mine and Michael's heartache to consider anymore. There was now a third person to consider.

Chapter 15
Reasonable Doubt
1994 - 1995

Once more I managed to time my return to England just as the winter was bedding in, leaving behind the promise of spring in the place which now felt more like home. I often wondered if this unfortunate clash of hemisphere seasons had conspired to make me suffer for my lesson of love even more than I had to!

James and I stayed with my parents briefly, because it proved difficult to find a flat as a single mother, and I thought it would buy me some time while I looked. Having a young baby in the house wasn't easy for them and the tension became palpable. It put more pressure on what was already a delicate relationship. We'd had sporadic contact over the last few years - I had distanced myself because of guilt and fear around my situation and then there had been the awkward goodbye at the airport when I was pregnant.

My situation felt so incongruous to how it's supposed to feel when a daughter shares her newborn with her parents. There was no air of celebration, no grandparent fussing. In their eyes I was the wayward daughter, who'd turned up with an illegitimate baby with some random boyfriend. But because I was hiding an even more shocking truth from them, I was extra defensive. I remember in the first day or so, James being in a bouncer chair. At that age babies need monitoring constantly. When I casually asked, 'Would you keep an eye on him while I have a shower?' I got the distinct impression that this was an imposition, rather than a grandmotherly joy.

I barely lasted a week before I called my cousin and poured out my predicament. He invited me to stay with him and his wife in Bristol while I figured out my life plan.

It was a perplexing time indeed. Despite my conviction that I was doing the right thing by leaving Michael, the reality of it felt all wrong. I knew he was suffering miserably back in Perth. We spoke daily, our love for each other never diminishing, and he told me that every day he sat in James's bedroom - the one he'd painted with *Paddington Bears* in bold colours just a few months earlier - and cried. It was still full of photos and memorabilia of our time together. He remembered it being full of giggles. And now, silence.

I remember one particularly emotional phone call. 'Sophia, please try to remember what we once thought was possible for us. Please consider whether we could regain trust in our relationship. Maybe we don't have to lose everything and we can make sense of it all.' I recognised how hard it was for him, finding a whole new routine without the people whom he had shared his home and routine with.

Every conversation went over the same questions as to how on earth we were going to live on opposite sides of the planet, with our hearts aching so much, and giving our son access to only one of his parents. It had seemed the only solution in the moment, but in actuality, it had transpired to be no solution at all. We hadn't meant to break our happy home. All we wanted was to be free to be together. Why, oh why, did we have to go through this pain?

Michael often wrote poetry. He loved to express both his joy and anguish this way. Here is one such poem he sent to me during this period.

My missing muse…
Oh! When..? When to rage and curse as fate betrays...?
Whilst I'm preoccupied for endless days
In missing your sweet heart and shining soul...
Or when? to philosophise, seeking help from ancient
proverbs told..?

Or, shall fatalism stab my hope to death...
When each word from you had so quickly stopped my breath...!
And so, to prayer, last night my aching heart had led...
And today! Your long-lost, searched for, fallen note was rescued from the floor,
By kind destiny on the far side of my bed...!!
The instinct and belief had never ever left my head,
That rescued, I too, one day would be,
When I found the soulmate angel, who had so long looked for me...
The lioness of love and trust, whom my heart hoped would find my door!
Her female compass and my telepathy...
Had found me waiting...
And brought her home, to set me free.

***

James was too young for me to go to work, so I stayed with him all day, every day; the empty days rolled into one. I felt desperately sad for him too, missing out on a relationship with his father.

My cousin introduced me to a divorced friend, hoping a date may cheer me up and help me move on. He was a nice man, and we went for a few walks with James in his pushchair followed by nice lunches. But all I could think about was being together as a family with Michael. Opening my heart to another man was incomprehensible.

I coped with two months of this painful existence before I caved in to the desire to be with my greatest love. Once more I found myself boarding a plane for yet another long-haul flight around the world. Michael was everything to me. Kind, generous, intelligent, inventive, funny, loving. I knew now that I had to show James how much his parents loved each other and loved him. I knew I was doing the right thing, even in the absence of any clarity of what the future held.

I can't describe the joy and relief at being reunited at Perth airport with James in my arms. The smell of Michael's familiar aftershave; the reassuring warmth of his embrace; and the love and tenderness shining in his eyes confirmed to me that I was home, and come what may, we would find a way through.

The three of us spent a beautiful day in one of our favourite parks. When we put James to bed in his familiar wooden cot, we both shed tears as we acknowledged the emotional toll that the last two months had taken.

I arrived just in time for Christmas and for the long-awaited opening, in January, of his magnificent new office, which was marked with a champagne reception.

Michael employed me again to front the reception desk two days a week, and I put James in a local nursery, which he loved. Now that Michael had a space to be proud of, he would invite all his clients in for meetings. The place soon became a bustling environment – a signature of Michael's personality. I loved meeting the wealthy interesting clients, many of them endearingly eccentric. I even took an interior design course because I wanted to add my own creative input to clients' special new homes. It gave me such job satisfaction when they took on one of my design ideas.

We both threw ourselves full force into making it the most well-known bespoke architecture firm in the area. We made a great, professional team - if I do say so myself! Although Michael now had several architects on the payroll, many clients only wanted his name on their drawings. They had learned of his reputation for eagle-eyed detail and warmed to his enthusiastic manner. While he worked long hours to accommodate this demand, I busied myself by rejoining the mother and baby group and going on long walks with the other mums and toddlers.

To me, James seemed incredibly bright compared to other children, though I'm sure every mum believes that. Michael and I often marvelled at how quickly he picked things up and how switched on he was. With his huge blue eyes and bright blond hair, I was convinced he was the most handsome baby I'd ever seen, and ridiculously photogenic!

We celebrated his first Christmas in 1994 with a BBQ with the couple who knew the truth about our situation. Michael bought me a stunning *Longines* watch, with an engravement on the back…*Dear Sophia, anytime at all…Love Michael Xmas 1994.* I still have it now, thirty years later, and it looks as good as new. It always reminds me that even through the heartbreak and disappointment; even though I may have changed my view on the rights and wrongs of our relationship over the years, we did share many happy moments.

A couple of months later, when his first birthday came around, we celebrated it at a local tennis club with other parent friends who were completely oblivious to the upheaval we'd just gone through.

I noticed he looked blotchy that afternoon and then became aware that his temperature had soared. It looked like he had chicken pox. The timing was far from the ideal, just as he was surrounded by lots of other toddlers. The spots covered every inch of his little body which is an unusual manifestation of this virus. We took him to the local walk-in clinic and the duty doctor was totally perplexed and wanted to take pictures of him. It turned out it wasn't chicken pox, but *erythema infectiosum*, which is much worse and presents with a high temperature and runny nose. James coped with the discomfort stoically and to our relief, none of his birthday party guests came down with it.

During his recovery from this illness, we both went into his room one morning to find him standing sturdily on two feet in his cot, fully alert, gurgling happily as he watched us enter. Michael turned to me, open-mouthed, 'See that?' he gasped. 'That stance, so upright, in that babygrow. This is the vision I had of him in my dream when you were pregnant!'

I was blown away. I remembered Michael talking about that dream when we worried about the DNA risks during my pregnancy. This auspicious moment served to reassure me that James and I were very much destined to be here.

***

Our idyllic life ticked on, and we were both incredibly happy. When we had time off, we went for weekends away - walking or camping. We enjoyed our quirky little garden that Michael had spent weeks landscaping. There was a crooked lemon tree which bore fat juicy fruit, and Michael installed trellis with exotic foliage, bamboo, and jasmine. We decorated it with fairy lights, candles and garden mirrors, which made it magical in the evenings in all seasons.

If it weren't for our secret, we would have had the dream life that any two lovers could wish for. But we did have our secret. And it gnawed at my insides whenever I thought of my parents or how the long-term future would unfold. We were living in a bubble, yet to be popped by exposure. The reality outside our bubble had not changed, no matter how much richer the inside of it had become. Our relationship, if exposed, would be considered incestuous and punishable by law, and derided and shamed socially.

It seemed so cruel and unjust that we cared for our son, we cared for each other, I even cared for others in my chosen vocation - everything we did came from the heart, yet we lived in fear of being condemned if people knew of our biological connection. Before James, I never stopped wrestling with the anomaly that our love could feel so right, bring so much joy and yet be considered so wrong. Now that I had James, there was another unanswerable question: how could our darling boy's life - so happy and vibrant - that blessed us in every way, be considered a crime? But the law was the law, and we were breaking it. I struggled with that knowledge day in and day out.

One day, Michael burst home from the office desperate to tell me something.

'I think I can get a DNA test,' he said.

'How?' I asked. We had considered the possibility of a DNA test before but rule it out because such a sophisticated thing seemed only available in crime films.

'I have a client who is a doctor. He asked about James and for some reason I mentioned I had another daughter – out there somewhere. We got onto the subject of Janet's pregnancy and confusion over dates. He said I should do a DNA test. He has some in his surgery. They are quite the new thing apparently.'

'He doesn't suspect anything does he?' I asked urgently. It seemed too good to be true.

'Of course not. I said my daughter is in England.'

'Then let's do it. It could be the salvation of us.' I agreed. It had been a long time since we had entertained the desperate hope that we may not be related; Since those endless circular conversations theorising about whether Janet may have slept with someone else.

Now, I thought, we would get our definitive answer, which was both exciting and terrifying. We had everything to gain or lose. If the test came back negative, it would release us to live and love without fear or guilt. But if it came back positive, there could be no more hoping. It would confront us with the stark reality of the consequences for our future.

Within a week, we had the test. We snipped off some strands of hair and swabbed our mouths and sent our samples off. We prayed with all our hearts for a reprieve - for a miracle. However, we both suspected, though were reluctant to admit it, that our powerful connection and recognition of each other's qualities was because we were related. To hope for this not to be true was clutching at straws. That we knew.

We waited weeks for the results. I felt in limbo, like quietly waiting to see if the eye of a storm would come right for us or pass over us. 'Please, please, please may it be negative,' I prayed. For some periods, I allowed myself to fantasise about waking up from this nightmare, and for once I experienced a light-heartedness that had been missing for so long. But then the worry would return. In my heart of hearts I knew. We knew.

I remember the day the envelope arrived. Hands shaking, heart pounding, I tore it open and within seconds my eyes fell on the result.... 99.9% chance of positive paternity. Why we felt so devastated, I don't really know. Perhaps it was because the truth was immortalised, in ink, in front of us, and there was no more denying it. All my anxieties about the future which I'd been holding back like a damn, now flooded back in. It was devastating confirmation of our doomed plight.

'This really does change things.' Michael said with a look of defeat. I looked at him expectantly before he said something which I never thought I'd hear his utter. 'Darling, this means we may have to separate.'

I was staggered because he had always believed in us unfalteringly. I didn't know whether he meant these words. It was always he who held the faith. But perhaps in this moment, the magnitude of all the very possible consequences flooded his mind.

Chapter 16

The Discovery

1995

A dark cloud hung over us in the days and weeks that followed. James was flourishing. He was such a joy, yet my heart ached when I thought of what may lie ahead for us. The test results kept haunting me, reminding me of the prospect that we may have to part.

On the other hand, I missed my friends and extended family members, who I'd left behind in England. I longed more and more to open up to them about my life as a new mum. I kept thinking how Michael's brother, sister and parents would never be able to visit; Or how we would ever manage family gatherings. My parents showed no inclination to come all the way to Australia to visit, but I would have to visit them at some point and how could I keep a whole side of my life with Michael a secret from them and pretend I was a single mum?

They continued to write to me weekly and send baby clothes and presents, and I sent regular photos to them of James. But I felt sad not to be able to tell them that I was with the father of my child and that we were all so happy and well. Michael, always looking to fulfil his creative flair, took hundreds of stunning shots of James and me; but I could never send those pictures to my parents because they would wonder why they looked so professional and who took them.

We even became concerned about James calling Michael 'daddy', in preparation for when they did inevitably meet him. We began referring to him as 'Mikey' so he would copy us. It breaks my heart to think about it.

Until now, we had always believed, to our core, that we weren't doing anything wrong. We clung to the excuse that we didn't know we were related for sure, perhaps kidding ourselves that if we knew definitively that we were related, we would stop. Now we had that definitive knowledge, we had to face this obligation to reconsider our future. Michael himself had said in the past that if we ascertained a positive DNA test, it would relinquish any hope of defence should we be accused by authorities of carrying on an incestuous relationship. 'It would be no life for you if you couldn't be carefree and confident,' he had said, but I never took these cautionary words seriously because DNA tests were the stuff of science fiction.

We briefly entertained the idea of moving to South America and living off-grid and merely existing together – happily. But it was just fantasy talk. We knew that wouldn't be practical and Michael said he could never live with himself if I lost all connections with my friends and family because we were running from the law.

Day in day out, I obsessed about how on earth we were going to sustain our life together veiled in secrecy. Michael fluctuated between being resolute in his belief that we could make it through somehow, as long as we were true to our love and stuck together; and then being defeatist about our future following the DNA test and resigning himself to separation. We had always shared the same concerns, but Michael had always had more conviction in his direction than me. He was more resourceful and independent in his analysis, which equated to a stronger sense of self. He would always assure me that even if people did find out, they would eventually lose interest, and we would be left alone to get on with our lives when they saw how happy we were as a family. He had the confidence to face what he saw as short-term consequences; He had faith that people would see us as good people and we would win compassion and understanding. But now, this steadfast belief was wavering. Ultimately neither of us could cast off the anxiety and fear that, at best, we'd lose our network of friends; worse, be arrested; or most terrifying of all, have James taken from us.

All these concerns were juxtaposed against our real-life experience, which was that each and every person whom we had dared share our story with had been entirely sympathetic and supportive.

In a bid to quell my fears, I decided to go to the library to search for textbooks or articles about adoption. I didn't know exactly what this research mission would provide. Perhaps I was just looking for clues which could help explain our plight. What I ended up discovering, however, was a vital piece of information, which laid the foundations for me to process my story, and which later sparked my intention to write this book.

I typed in: 'Adoption feelings of attraction' and an academic article popped up about a new but disputed phenomenon in the adoption community known as Genetic Sexual Attraction (GSA).

When I registered the words, I read on eagerly. It turned out there was growing acceptance of this concept. The author described it as a common psychological reaction to the extreme emotions of reunion and proclaimed that it was more commonplace than previously acknowledged.

The author wrote, in words to the effect, that GSA should not be viewed as a sexual deviance or an emotional disorder, but rather should be understood as a consequence of genetic likeness, and a powerful yearning for intimacy and connection between two people who have been separated for their whole lives. This yearning can be experienced and expressed as intensely emotional. It feels very much like falling in love. The article went as far as stating that once in motion, the feelings are 'unstoppable'. Many UK adoption agencies were apparently waking up to this phenomenon and starting to include it in their risk management counselling.

My heart raced at the prospect that there could be others out there who could empathise with what we were going through. At last, there was something to which I could clutch, to make sense of my deep angst.

Now I had this term as a lead, I continued searching and found other media articles and academic papers mentioning Genetic Sexual Attraction. I learned that the term was coined in the US in the late 1980s by Barbara Gonyo, an amateur artist living in Chicago. In her 40s, she met the twenty-something son she gave up for adoption and found herself feeling and behaving as if she were falling in love with him. She was unable to get him out of her mind and became desperate to spend as much time with him as possible. When she sought help and spoke to others about her feelings, she found she was far from alone. She managed to attract the interest of academics and researchers, and it is thanks to her that this phenomenon was put on the map. She founded *Truth Seekers in Adoption* in 1991, a support group where adoptees and their newfound relatives could discuss their experiences and struggles with people who shared similar situations, without fear of condemnation.

However, it also became clear that there was much debate over the terminology. Genetic Attraction, Genetic Romantic Attraction and Intra-familial Love were some of the alternatives.

In this story, I choose to refer to it as Genetic Attraction (GA). I omit the 'S' because from my experiences, and others I've spoken to in the years since, the bond that the term refers to is not primarily sexual. Far from it. It is the 'sexual' part of the label which I fear is responsible for the underlying shame and distress associated with it.

One consensus about this phenomenon – whatever terminology the experts used – was that it was far removed from incest, as society understands that to be. Professionals in the adoption field were keen to point out that the attraction commonly experienced between reunited relatives almost never occurs among adoptive families who've lived together when the adoptee was a child. Some voices were – and still are - pushing for change in the way GA relationships were defined and dealt with. 'Incest' is still punishable by law in almost all modern societies, and since the people who get caught up in GA suffer enough, these experts argued, their pain shouldn't be compounded by being branded criminals.

I also read that those who have experienced GA describe a magnetic force and uncontrollable feelings like nothing they've ever experienced in love before. Men and women talk about an overpowering, almost electric grip of emotion, an inability to keep away from the other person and an instinctive sense of 'belonging' together.

One article suggested that the romantic love that develops - particularly when mothers meet their adult children for the first time – mirrors the sensuous bonding between a new mother and her baby. The theory is that both regress to a very early stage of the baby's development. A relationship between mother and baby could be considered sensual in many respects, but we wouldn't dream of calling it 'romance' or 'being in love' when it's breastfeeding, cradling and stroking - or when it's a mother and baby gazing into one another's eyes. The feelings of attraction when these adult individuals meet again or for the first time can mimic the mother and baby intensity. It can be so overwhelming, so great, so deep that it can express as a yearning to become as physically and emotionally close as possible, or even a craving for sexual intimacy.

I was struck by how GA seemed to cross age, cultural and even sexuality boundaries. There have been cases of heterosexual brothers meeting and having an intimate experience; or sisters; or mothers and daughters, even though they'd never felt same-sex attraction with anyone before.

I don't know how long I was in the library for, but it felt like a veil had been lifted and I could see more clearly. Many times, Michael and I had asked ourselves if we were being narcissistic, wanting to love our own mirror image, but that's not how we felt. Yes, we saw qualities in each other that we could identify with, and strong physical attributes that we admired, but when we were together, it didn't feel at all as though we were 'family'. Now that I knew GA was a thing, it provided relief that we were not crazy or deviant in any way. This had been entirely predictable!

However, in the days and weeks that followed, it also slowly dawned on me that if we had known about GA before we met, with support and the appropriate counselling, we may have been able to identify our overwhelming feelings, bring them under control and establish an orthodox father-daughter bond. The light relief, provided by the discovery of the well-documented concept of GA gave way to some indignance that I had not been warned about it.

Michael and I had got so deeply involved, so quickly, that only an official warning label could have had any chance to stop us. Because we felt that our experience was unique to us, we couldn't imagine talking to anyone about it. Nor could we imagine stopping loving each other.

Where would we be now, if we had been enlightened on this?

***

I tried to get on with life without letting the turbulence of our latest discoveries distract me. Michael's 49th birthday came around and we flew to Sydney and watched *Phantom of the Opera* at the iconic Opera House overlooking the harbour. In my lovely evening dress and Michael looking handsome in black tie, I was able to forget all my cares for the night and return to enjoying the magic of just being together. Even through this worrying time, he still made me laugh and still transmitted his positive energy to whatever we were doing. I remember that evening well, laughing and feeling great.

But this reprieve from our troubles was not to last long. Shortly after that trip, I stumbled upon an article which shook me to the core. A national newspaper reported on a couple in a similar situation to ours: A daughter, separated from her father through her parents' divorce when she was just three months old, was reunited with him when she was a young adult and they fell in love. She had two children from a previous marriage, and through this new romance with her biological father, went on to have a little girl. They were reported to social services when the father's ex-wife found out. Police swooped in on their home in a dawn raid and took all the children into custody.

Her two older teenage children knew the truth and were interviewed by police and put into care while the case was investigated. On the date the article was published, all the children were in foster care.

I was beside myself. Suddenly my angst at being castigated by friends was superseded by a much graver terror – losing James. I became paranoid about all the people to whom we had revealed our true story. What if they ever had a gripe with us? They could easily report us. What if they told someone, who then told someone else….?

Returning to England again – although a barren prospect – felt like a beacon for safety. When I told Michael about the article, he expressed immense sorrow for this couple. He was often a tearful person when it came to other people's afflictions, as he had great capacity for empathy, and he shed a tear now for this couple, who were so like us. He found this very sobering. It was a stark reminder that our relationship was complex and there could be repercussions – legally or personally.

I eagerly looked out for updates on this story. A few weeks later one emerged, revealing that the children had been returned to the couple. Authorities concluded that all three siblings were happy and well cared for and there was no reason to separate them from their parents. They were allowed to continue to live together as a family.

They did press interviews, unashamed of their choice to identify as a couple, hiding their reality from no one. I was full of admiration for how they stood up for themselves and got on with their lives.

It was heartening to hear that they had come through this

harrowing experience, but the ridicule they endured because of it was disturbing and I knew that if it came down to it, I would not have the same courage to speak so openly about a relationship that invites such censor and condemnation.

I took some solace in the fact that after a high-profile case like that in the public arena, it might prompt more research or discussion and help bring about a new level of understanding. But I also knew that was a far-fetched dream because it was an isolated case and the truth was, the experiences of others in GA relationships remained obscure due to the reluctance to admit to them.

It was inevitable that within a few short weeks, I became yet again overwhelmed with uncertainty and worry. Try as I might, I could not calm the internal storm that raged within me. I would often wake up in the middle of the night and, unable to sleep again, would go into the lounge and sit and pray for guidance. I called on my faith in the divine source of love to guide me. 'Damned if we do, and damned if we don't,' was what I kept thinking. My head spun with indecision.

I kept flitting between the decision: Leave or stay. Stick or twist, as if we were playing poker. Each time I changed my mind, it was with enough conviction that I was prepared to uproot my whole life to another country. What a crazy roller coaster ride it was. Would I ever be able to get off it and stop spinning?

It was an impossible situation for Michael too. It pained him to know how much I was struggling. Of course, he tried all he could to allay my fears, but he acknowledged that it would be wrong to try and stop me. Ultimately, he was aware that it was my decision whether I stayed in Australia with him or started a new life without him back home. Bearing in mind that my decision would impact whether he lost his son, it was all the more indicative of his determination to put my welfare first. Looking back, I appreciate how incredibly brave and honourable he was. Facing head-on the prospect that his life was about to crumble, he still protected my emotions first, always reassuring me that whatever path I took, it would be ok.

James and I eventually left in July 1995, when he was 15 months old. Very chatty by this time, and devoted to his dear 'Mikey', it was heartbreaking to see them embrace and say goodbye at the airport. I didn't know how to explain to this little boy that we were going away and that his Mikey wasn't coming with us. Michael strained to hold back tears. He bravely smiled and whispered gentle words of reassurance to his son.

Since then, I've seen and read how fathers suffer when their children are taken from them. Because a mother is considered the main carer, sole custody is commonly given to her. My heart bleeds thinking of the anguish and loss that Michael endured - powerless to affect the situation; resigned to a life of quiet desperation; sitting at home alone in the evenings pining for his beloved family. The absence of sounds from me and James chattering and laughing, would amplify the deafening silence that engulfed him.

I'm crying as I write this, even now, 30 years later, as I remember the agony of that goodbye. For me, having James gave me strength, and a purpose to carry on. But how Michael survived it, I have no idea. I can only conclude that by now, we were no strangers to sorrow, and we could go through the motions like robots.

Michael, in his forlorn state, wrote a letter in the days after I left. It is one of the few remaining ones I still have. Below is an extract, which I want to share because it captures his experience in this unfolding story.

> *July 1995*
>
> *Friday*
>
> *My whole heart, soul and being seemed to trail through those opening and closing steel doors, as I saw you and James slip out of sight. I was proud of you. So brave, and yet frail and full of so much feeling. The airport rang slowly around me in a numb and unreal way, like the scene of a bomb blast, and I moved mechanically, controlling my body so I looked natural and normal,*

feeling self-conscious, with every step towards the observation bar and lounge.

I could see Gate 5 seemed quite a long way, and I hoped you weren't having to rush, or be worried, or stressed soon. I imagined your feelings inside as you tried to stow the baby carriage. Perhaps the stewardess would take it for you. I felt numb with an ache in my tummy, like a famine. A beer seemed questionable, but I took one, and some cashews and watched with a swooning, distant irritation as two staff fussed and fiddled to put the nuts in the bowl and get my change.

I looked at the plane and wanted to go and pull you both off it. All the scenarios ran around my head like a collage of intense but abstract theatre. My distraction kept returning to the cabin windows, and I was aware that it was unrealistic to be cross with myself that I hadn't thought of bringing two of those little red torches, so that we could have shone them at each other; to know to see where the heart and the tears and the loss and the person we each loved was, exactly. I remembered how sad and long my stay at the airport was last time, when I videoed the plane standing, then the taxiing, and then take-off from a distance, and then I decided to go.

The day was a stranger to me, blank and anonymous and indifferent. The light was plain and the sky featureless. Everything looked like a photograph taken accidentally, with no feature or focus or interest, except that it was simply there. I was worried or uncertain about going back to the house that would feel so empty and left behind, as though the light and power and gas and water had all been cut off: The house that you didn't like, but which we'd both always remember, so many events, so many phases, so many departures on outings and memories of weekends, leading step by step to this one.

The car seemed so neat, like a stranger's as I arrived. I realised it was sad and silly that we hadn't had two cars all along. In the house, I found the echoes of the last hours of packing and rushing and the beer that was left in the fridge. I started picking over everything, tidying this and that. There are two of James's last wet nappies to throw out. How impractical the vague thought was to even consider keeping one! I cleaned out the microwave shelf, and the plastic utensils cupboard, and old glassware, and made the kitchen sparse and neat. I collected all the little bits of James and kissed some of them as I stored them all in the David Jones perfume box with the red ribbon.

I put his name card on top and laid out the James letters in his cot, the little room filled with his bassinet, the Porta cot, the pram, the baby backpack and his yellow toy box full of balls and things he used to bang around. I continued to tidy the house until 14 hours later, at 4:30am, I fell into bed.

Saturday,

I didn't feel great. It was a bad night. I remembered your phone call from Hong Kong Airport. You were very brave. You are brave. You're good, and you're admirable, and you're a wonderful mum. I thought of little James lying in your arms, and then walking the aisles, looking up at his fellow travellers. I wished I was with you so you didn't have to carry everything at Heathrow, and so I could share international travel with my little boy, and the woman I love. I had a shower and remembered James splashing and watching me shave, just as I used to examine dad shaving long ago. He never puts shaving cream in his mouth anymore. Now he just plays with it, and carefully washes it all off his fingers and his tummy.

The next pages cover several diary-like entries of his next few days. He ended the letter by switching his address to James:

I look in your room every time I pass. I listen for your footsteps and the noises you make. I see your eyes and your smile, and I remember your morning kisses. I miss you and cry for every day lost between us. Look after your sweet mum and remember me. Do, please do, until I can hold you again.

Your sweet face, Michael

When I read this letter, once more I felt growing vexation that I had not been warned about the risks of genetic attraction when I started the search for my birth parents. Perhaps, if we had been made fully aware of the powerful, overwhelming feelings that can emerge when reuniting relatives come together, and we were supported through it, a full-blown romantic relationship might have been avoided.

It was from this grievance that the seed was sown for me to one day share my story. If this topic were brought out of the dark and into the public domain, I thought, it would make way for greater understanding and compassion for those whose lives have been devastatingly affected, like ours. Perhaps others like me, in the future, wouldn't be governed by fear of people's reactions. Better still, they would get the support they need to navigate the intense emotions before it becomes too late.

Chapter 17

Separation

1995

My cousin and his wife came to the rescue again for my temporary living arrangements. They found a holiday flat, owned by their friends, for me to rent near the seaside town of Weston-super-Mare. It was within easy reach of them in nearby Bristol.

My mum, ever supportive despite our recent rift, met James and me at the airport. She still had no idea what I was going through and was in the dark about her grandson's paternity. She must have presumed I had love troubles with the fictional 'Grant' in Australia, and I was coming home as a single mum. My parents loved me very much and I could tell that they were upset that I was in this predicament. I can't imagine how they would react if they knew the extent of my troubles.

Mum drove us all the way to the holiday let – a two-and-a-half-hour drive from Heathrow – and settled us in. This time, she was more engaged with her grandson. The many photographs I sent meant there were no surprises on his appearance. She cooed to him that he was a big boy now, and commented how blonde and blue-eyed he was, given that I was so dark.

But there was still the odd caustic remark, reminiscent of our rift. 'Are you *still* breast feeding?' Having never birthed her own child, I suppose she thought this act was something you do for a little bit and she didn't fully understand the bonding benefits that breastfeeding afforded, nor that it was recommended to do it for as long as possible, even into toddlerhood.

But actions speak louder than words, and she was brilliantly helpful, providing us with basic groceries when we arrived. After she settled us in, she set off for the long drive back to Yorkshire, leaving us to sleep. The solitude she left behind was notable. Here I was, alone with my little toddler in an unfamiliar town, in a soulless flat, with rudimentary furnishings, and no one to talk to about my situation. Perth was a vibrant, cosmopolitan city, and by comparison it was a shock to find myself in this sleepy suburb, without the familiar hustle and bustle that I was used to. Not to mention no Michael by my side to warm my heart and brighten my day.

The following morning, James woke up at 5am because of jet lag. I remember walking with him, trying not to act as subdued as I felt, to a nearby park while the early summer dawn was breaking but the night chill was still in the air. I pushed him on the swing as he gleefully chattered about the trees and ladybird he had spotted. The sweet, unfettered joy and enthusiasm of children is such a gift! My heart swelled with love for this little boy, lifting me momentarily out of my melancholy. I swore to be the best mum that I could be to him, and to protect him as best I could as we embarked on this next unchartered phase of our life together.

The separation was worse than before this time. It rang of permanence. It was even more devasting for Michael back home because of the empty silence that now saturated his home.

He told me that he felt like he was standing on the edge of a big, black hole that he feared he might fall into. Every morning, he went to work, put on his professional face and met with clients. Every evening, he returned to the lifeless rooms at home, where he ate his food and cried his tears alone. I had James to brighten my day and lighten my mood. He was my connection to Michael, which made my daily existence more bearable than his.

I was gripped with guilt about what I had done to this man, who had given me so much and helped me so much. But I had to pull myself together for James's sake, so I applied myself to the practical tasks needed to create a new life as a single mum with my beautiful boy. Michael supported us financially, so I didn't have to worry about finding rent, but I was still very conscious of spending his money. I found an old car that was just about reliable and bought a second-hand child car seat. I then set about the task of finding a more long-term rental property. I soon discovered that this area was far from the affluent part of town. It had a reputation for being the hangout area for some rather choice characters!

The estate agent I dealt with made me feel like a second-class citizen for being a single mother looking for a flat alone. He was an older guy, hardened and cynical and I just sensed his disrespect when I turned up with a child. I was looking at the lower end of the market, and it was clear that we weren't the priority when scheduling viewings. He was always quick to answer his mobile to his other clients when we were together and I observed his difference in tone with them. I'd never experienced this stigma before. It was quite an unpleasant awakening that this was my new reality - categorised as a less respected member of society.

I eventually found a flat with potential. It was in a down-market area of town, and was a bit grotty, but I could see from the layout that it could scrub up well with some decoration. How I now longed for Michael's artistic input!

A couple of days after we moved in, I was horrified when James and I both developed itchy, red bites on our legs, and then on our backs. They could only be fleas! I learned from the neighbours that before me, an alcoholic mum had lived there with her young daughter and had neglected the place.

When I told my mum about this, she sprang into action. She told me to source some new carpet and then she drove all the way across the country again to help me clean the place up. She was so practical like this. We may have been challenged in other areas of our relationship, but this was her way of showing devotion to me - her only daughter. Because of my dad's job, she'd moved our family many times and was well versed on what to do. She was a woman of action.

She stayed for several nights. We stripped the old carpet to find the underlay beneath falling apart – it was gross. We took it to the tip, laid new carpets, cleaned everywhere and painted all the stained walls. We made James's room the homeliest, adding colourful pictures and teddies. She was brilliant and I felt very supported.

Once I got our living situation sorted, I then set about the important issue of earning a living. I applied for a position as staff physiotherapist in the outpatient's department of a local private hospital and was offered the post, much to my relief. It wasn't that exciting. I was dealing with routine operation recoveries and it was a stark contrast to the glamour of the reception desk in Michael's flashy office. But I didn't have the strength to apply over and over again for more choice roles.

I found a decent day nursery for James and the semblance of a routine took shape. Our basic needs were met but I was far from content. I made an effort to speak to other residents in my building and instigated some social evenings in the communal garden. One couple, who lived upstairs, told me over a glass of wine that when I first moved in, they had a friend over to stay. He'd witnessed me carrying my furniture in and showed a keen interest in who I was. They confessed that they'd replied: 'A posh bird from Australia'. The friend pushed for an intro and so they brought him along to our next neighbourly drinks gathering. I remember him trying to talk to me all afternoon, but I was preoccupied with James and in no way interested in dating, so I was somewhat aloof.

My childhood friend Lisa came to visit me in those first weeks, and she recalls me being stressed, easily irritated and a shadow of the former friend with whom she had gone through adolescence and beyond. I don't remember this particular incident, but she reliably informs me that we went to a café and I was having trouble breast feeding James. I asked for some food that I could mash up for him, but the waiting staff didn't understand and brought out something totally unsuitable and I got cross. 'It was not like the sensible, fun and joyful person I knew.' She later told me.

I suppose I was still pining for the love and belonging I shared with Michael. It wasn't easy handling parent duties all alone when I wasn't used to it. I would be lying if I said I didn't feel the strain of this. Co-parenting with Michael had always been a joy. Managing all the responsibilities and decisions alone was not how I thought my life would be!

However, instead of the despair I felt during our other separations, I was more reflective this time. I was able to feel gratitude for the treasured times we had together, and for the rare experience of true love. I also acknowledged the huge relief since breaking away from my life there. Being removed from our impossible situation lifted me out of the constant fog of anxiety that had overshadowed my whole being for so long. I was now trying hard to restore a sense of stability in my life. I focused on the simple things in life - prioritizing James's needs and that was it. I could cope with that.

My first bit of excitement was getting signed up by a local model agency as a side hustle. I had to do a five-week diploma to learn catwalk technique and composure for photos (pre selfie-culture, such tricks were not common knowledge). I met a guy on this course and cautiously allowed myself a date or two. It didn't really go anywhere, but it was a milestone for me that I could even entertain the idea of romance with another man.

I soon felt upbeat enough to go out with friends and went out dancing, which I hadn't done for years. It was clear now that I was well on my way to building a new life without Michael by my side.

Chapter 18
Exposed
1996 - 1997

While I was busying myself with settling into my new life, communications between Michael and I became strained. This had never been the case before – we had always vibed together no matter what our moods or difficulties. But now, he was struggling with depression and because I felt so guilty for my role in inflicting this, I didn't know how to console him.

The tension built between us. He was holding on to the hope that we could find our way back to each other and be a family, but because I was now consciously putting my welfare first, I actively pushed him away. There was no going back for me. I had no choice but to keep him at arm's length even though it broke my heart to treat him coldly.

When the new year came around, he became desperate to see us again and pushed for a visit. 'It's six months! It's so hard not being able to imagine you both in your new surroundings,' he said sadly. Even though I knew this would set me back emotionally, I could not deny him seeing his son, so we agreed he would come and stay for three weeks. But I worried about what I would say to my new network about this Australian man staying with me. James still called Michael 'daddy', as well as 'Mikey', and he was bound to do that in front of people. What if my mum wanted to visit?

Michael was visibly both delighted and pained when he laid eyes on James. 'Look at what I've missed,' he said, referring to the big changes in James in the eight months that we'd been gone. I'd sent him so many photos, but it never quite matches up to seeing someone in the flesh. Our little boy was talking now, and his blonde hair was even thicker to touch. James still recognized his daddy when he saw him. The strong love bond between them was very much still present.

It was an antagonising time for us both. For Michael, seeing me with a job, settled into a rental flat, on friendly terms with the neighbours hammered home, with finality, that James and I weren't coming back this time.

Neither of us could deny that we were no longer a united front, doing battle together. We each had our own battles, neither sure how to support the other. At times, Michael expressed his disappointment that I couldn't find the courage to stick together and fight for our love. Through everything, we had always pledged to find a way. He said I was now allowing fear to take hold of me, instead of believing in the power of love to triumph, as he did.

At the time, his words killed me to hear. Letting him down was the last thing I ever wanted to do. But I knew that deep down, he knew I had to make this decision. I put any hurtful words down to his unfettered emotions of despair getting the better of him. He felt powerless as he witnessed me slipping away, taken by the tidal wave of fear and doubt.

A week's ski holiday together in France, capturing the late season snow, was meant to ease the atmosphere between us. James spent his second birthday in ski school, and Michael and I shared some moments of wonder seeing him so confident on his tiny skis. But when those moments passed, the strain was still in the air. Romantically, I had fully withdrawn, trying to protect myself from the pain. Yet it was hard to keep pushing away the man who loved me so much; whom I still loved; who had shown me so much generosity and given me so much fulfilment.

We had rows that holiday – hardly surprising of any ex-couple attempting to have a happy holiday together. Michael was his usual gregarious self, chatting to everyone. Only, the altitude, jet lag and recent stress proved to be a lethal mix with *apres ski* alcohol. One night I got angry at him for staying out late and getting drunk. Another time, I got chatted up at an *apres* bar, by a charming French skier. Michael was not happy about it and we argued. I shouted at him that he was jealous and he needed to let me live. He was heartbroken, tired, tormented. But while we may have lashed out from stress, we always knew we were there for each other – not romantically anymore, but like family.

When we returned to the UK, I drove the three of us to Birmingham to pay a visit to Michael's extended family. They had never met James nor me. It was on the premise that I, his long-lost daughter, was a single mum with a toddler; and Michael was the grandad! Despite us no longer being together, there was still a connected energy about us. I was sure they could see it. But no one asked any awkward questions. Michael's sister had a baby of a similar age, and it pained Michael beyond words that he could not tell her that this was his son too. How we managed it, I do not know.

This was the first time I met my paternal grandmother (Michael's mother). She was a loving, grandmotherly figure. She showed her affection by cooking abundant, wholesome food but didn't ask any deep and personal questions. She had known of my existence because of Janet contacting her when she was pregnant with me – in desperation that somehow they could financially support her so she wouldn't have to give up her child.

It was a massive house with several wings - the same house where Michael and Janet sneaked into his father's study with cardinal urges all those years ago! I could tell my grandfather had been a revered professor. He loved to sit in an armchair, smoking or sucking a Werther's Original sweet, steering conversations onto the day's newspaper and politics. After that visit, my newly instated grandmother took an interest in James and me – their long-lost grandchild and great grandchild. She sent presents and birthday cards to both of us after our visit. She was wonderful.

***

When the day came around for Michael to return to Australia, there was a look of defeat in his eyes that I'd never seen before. He knew he had failed to win me back. I was riddled with guilt, and I couldn't help but question whether there was truth in his desperate words – had I lacked the courage to fight for us?

But no. I had to find faith in myself, in my own convictions, and do my best to move on with my life even though I continued to carry the burden of guilt for the pain I had caused him.

Shortly after his visit, my mum invited me out to lunch. This was unusual - my mum rarely suggested one-on-ones just to be social. We met in a country pub, at a halfway point between where we lived. I was nervous as I arrived. I knew something was up. We sat outside in the beer garden and I chatted about my life. She seemed uninterested in my trivia though, like she had an agenda.

And then the inevitable question arrived.

'Come on Sophia, who is James's father?'

I had dreaded this inevitable day. For years, I must have appeared cagey when talking about my time in Australia. God knows how I found the words, but I came clean.

'I knew it!' She cried, 'I told dad and aunty Sally that I thought it was Michael's baby. They wouldn't believe it but I knew it didn't add up.'

To my surprise, she was calm. She wasn't exactly sympathetic, but she didn't chastise me, or get angry or tearful. Any animosity was directed towards Michael, who she perceived as the enabler of this most unhealthy relationship. She saw me – her little girl– as the victim.

My mum inevitably relayed our conversation to my dad and gradually, the whole extended family was told. I am grateful to my mum for protecting me from any of their reactions. If anyone did voice disapproval, I didn't know about it. No one called me to speak about it. She, however, made it very clear what she thought of Michael. She called it abuse, which pained me greatly because it highlighted how misunderstood our love was. I didn't blame her for her reaction. The whole saga was very distressing, and she later told me that she went to the GP and was prescribed with antidepressants.

The fact that my wider family now knew, emboldened me to tell some of my new local friends too. But I soon learned that some found it too juicy to keep to themselves. I particularly regret telling one new friend, much younger than me. She had told me a story about something personal in her life over a glass of wine, and I reciprocated with mine, which I immediately realised was way out of proportion. A few weeks later, when I told my story to a more established friend, she informed me, 'Sophia, more people know about this than you realise.' Immediately I knew the source of this apparent spread of information.

All the old hallmarks of stress from guarding a secret returned as I began to wonder who knew and who didn't. Every time I met a friend, I would always think: 'Do they know?' 'Did I tell them? Have they heard on the grapevine?' I wished I hadn't told anyone. In hindsight I should have been more conscientious and monitored who I told this important secret to, but it was my nature to go with the flow of life, sharing intimate things when the moment felt appropriate.

Once the confession was out, there were a plethora of new challenges to come, which I was to soon discover would change relations dramatically between me, my family and Michael.

***

Unbeknown to me, my family was plotting to get Michael out of my life for good. They found the whole thing distressing and having never met him, nor seen us together, they had quickly concluded that he was irresponsible. He was the one who had the power to put the brakes on our relationship all those years ago. He was the one who should have known better. He was an astute businessman. Knowing the strength of their conviction on which they collaborated, I struggled to defend Michael. They wouldn't have listened to me. Unchallenged, their prejudice and anger towards him accumulated as time went by.

I, meanwhile, was trying to get on with my life, slowly finding new interests. I busied myself by reviving my interest in photography with an evening course. It wasn't lost on me that this was one of Michael's passions and I wondered again about the link between genes and our tendencies and interests in life.

I checked out fitness classes too, which led to an unrelated auspicious event. I wandered into a local crystal shop advertising yoga classes. I had noticed this shop before and felt a draw to it. Having always been curious about the meaning of life, my interest in alternative therapies and spirituality had grown stronger with all the challenges I'd faced over the last decade. I took my time, browsing all the interesting nicknacks in the shop. 'Colour therapy. What's that?' I asked a man with a beard who emerged from one of the rooms. He looked intently at me for a moment before explaining what it was.

Then he said, 'You have a son, don't you?'

'Yes.' I replied, expecting him to say his child goes to nursery with him, or something.

'He has blonde hair, and very blue eyes, doesn't he?'

'Yes.' I said, wondering how on earth he could possibly know that.

'I can see him. This boy is special. It's his last time here and he's been sent as your teacher.'

I don't remember what I replied, but I remember him smiling knowingly before disappearing back into his room. I later learned he was a practicing psychic. Seemingly he was getting a vision from the spiritual world when we conversed. I was baffled and didn't really know what to do with this information, so I chose to brush it aside and carried on as usual. But it's something that has always stuck with me and many times since, as James's love, wisdom and insights beyond his years have continually amazed me, I've thought to myself, 'Wow, that guy was right, James is my teacher!'

Sometime towards the end of 1996, continuing with my quest to embed myself fully into my new life, I saw a job advert in the local paper for independent distributors for a health food brand. I wanted to get on board and I successfully applied. I went to Blackpool for the launch event, excited by the prospect to put on a long black evening dress. I felt great! I was standing at the side of the large ballroom taking photos when the compare and entertainer approached and started chatting. He looked young but was charismatic and incredibly handsome. I didn't want to assume he was flirting, but when he asked for my number, it was obvious. I gladly gave it to him, and he rang a few days later. We talked for three hours! He had a lovely voice and was very engaging. We had a few more long evening phone calls, sometimes just listening to music together, swapping favourite artists. Then he asked if he could take me out and we started seeing each other.

Marcus was his name. He had a glamorous life in London as a presenter, writer and entertainer. Having been a child actor, he had lots of connections in showbusiness. He told me he was 28, and even though I was 32, I found him mature and intelligent. He made me laugh and we got on well. He pursued me enthusiastically, which I was flattered by because he was well aware I had a toddler, and I lived hours away from him. He could have had the choice of any gorgeous twenty-something in London, I was sure!

The first time I stayed over with Marcus in his modern bachelor pad on the Kings Road, I got a babysitter for James. I hated it, but I was desperate to have some fun and assured myself that he would be fine and that he was being looked after by a fully vetted and qualified minder. The next morning, rushing back on the train, I remember thinking, 'How will this ever work? I can't keep leaving James with babysitters!'

But it did work, for several months. He came out west to visit me a few times and I took James to London. Marcus was great with him and once took us to Hamleys, the huge toy store, and bought him an amazing magic kit, which he was completely enamoured with. Marcus had been a magician in his early career, and he spent hours with James showing him how to perform the tricks with flare!

Dating someone younger than me was strange after the 18-year upwards age-gap with Michael, but it was also quite refreshing. Marcus got picked up by chauffeurs and frequented fancy members clubs in London. I remember going to the cocktail bar on the fourth floor of Harrods and he played the piano and sang for me. It was really something! I was starting to feel some of the old joyful me return, starting to breathe in life again.

After a couple of months, I dared, after a long chat about life and its complexities, to tell him my story. He was totally unphased. He was kind and understanding and passed absolutely no judgement- a reaction I must say has been common among whomever I've told since, except ironically, from my family.

One thing that I was starting to realise was that when the concept of a GA relationship is received as a stand-alone story, without any context or details of the people involved, it is easily judged or condemned. But when I told my story to people who knew me, my good nature and my open heartedness, they received it with deep compassion and sympathy for the painful and sad human saga that was our love story.

Chapter 19

Daring to Love Again

1997 – 1998

I got my first taste of freedom from the daily emotional angst of the past few years through dating Marcus. I never expected we would be serious, but we shared an easy camaraderie, he was kind, fun and supportive and it was just the tonic I needed. We had many happy times, and he continued to give attention to James, understanding that he was my priority. Knowing that he knew my story and loved me anyway was liberating for me. I began to relax tentatively into the idea that perhaps my life wasn't ruined after all, and I could begin to heal from the pain and secrecy of the past.

Michael had conceded that we were now living in separate worlds. We still spoke regularly, and he told me he had also allowed himself to move on and meet someone. She was called Natalie, and they had met on a blind date, set up by a friend. She was younger than him and had a young girl of a similar age to James (now three).

I suppose it was inevitable that the time would come for him to ask if he could have James to stay with him in Perth. At first, I was resistant to the idea. I could not imagine my life without my little boy to look after. But Michael pointed out that there was not much time left before his school years began, and he wanted to make the most of this free time. When I had chance to consider this request, I reasoned it would be unfair to refuse. How could I deny James and his daddy time together? It would do James the world of good to spend time with his father - the male hero in his life. Also, it would afford me some freedom to spend more time with Marcus and experience being childfree for a while. The time will fly by, I reassured myself.

We agreed that Michael would fly over to collect James in December 1997, whisk him off for an Australian Christmas and New Year, and return him three months later, just before he turned four.

In the November before that, as the one-year anniversary of dating Marcus approached, he announced he had something to tell me. What followed came as quite a shock. He revealed that he was in fact five years younger than he previously disclosed. He was only 23, not 28! I found this hard to get my head around. Not for one minute had I suspected his real age as he was so confident and mature.

I don't think he had lied to me with questionable intention – he simply didn't want me to be put off by his age. He genuinely felt older than his years after his rich life experiences in the TV world. It was an interesting lesson for me in non-judgement. I had reacted to his 'secret', and I corrected myself to look at the context and the person involved, just as he had been able to do with my 'secret'. I understood why being thought of as older worked for him in a positive way. Although I forgave him for misleading me, he was still only 23! I was then 32, and after being with Michael, who was 18 years older, it was too much to deal with. I also knew that we didn't have a future together. I wanted to become a mum again at some point, and Marcus would definitely not be wanting a baby for a least a few years, so after an open an honest discussion, I ended the relationship.

After the initial rawness subsided, we settled into a friendship that lasted many years. It was only after he moved abroad many years later, with his new wife that our communication dwindled.

The timing of this breakup turned out to be a fortuitous twist of fate. The very week we called it, Marcus and I had been planning to go to a black-tie ball together for his birthday. That obviously wasn't going to happen now, so I found myself going with friends instead of a plus-one.

Standing in my long black velvet dress, halfway through the evening, from across the room I recognised a face I'd seen before. It was an attractive face, and I tried to hurry my brain into recalling where we might have met. Then it dawned on me. It was Andrew, from the neighbourly drinks in our communal garden. He was the friend of the neighbour, who'd commented on me carrying furniture when I moved in.

He approached and to my surprise I felt a wave of shyness. After chatting a little, he offered to buy me a drink, and then we had a dance.

'I'd like to take you out.' He said, a little shyly. 'It's a bit embarrassing, but I'm here with someone else tonight. It isn't a thing. We just met. I've promised to take her home, but can I take your number?'

He called me a few days later and we arranged a date. Things moved quickly this time. In contrast to Marcus, we came from similar backgrounds. He'd been to boarding school and came from a well-to-do family. He'd lost a parent to illness as a young boy, and one of his brothers was adopted so we had unusual family backgrounds in common. We were soon enamoured with each other.

He was a calming influence on me. After Marcus, who lived the high life in all the glamorous bars in the trendy parts of London; and Michael, with his high-energy eccentricity and creative chaos at home, Andrew was conventional and orderly. His house was tidy; he was always on time; he was practical, softly spoken and gentlemanly. He had risen through the conventional corporate ranks to become a CEO of a large printing company, which he seemed perfectly satisfied with.

One of his many hobbies was motorbiking. He'd pick me up on his huge Harley Davidson bike and we'd whizz along the country roads, me clinging tightly around his waist, loving every minute of it. He was a safe and competent rider, and I found riding tandem thrilling with the wind on my face, taking in the beautiful scenery flashing by. The first time he came over to mine,

James was in bed and I had a babysitter in situ, so they didn't have chance to meet. Then, within two weeks of us dating, Michael flew in from Australia to take James back as we agreed.

It was painful seeing Michael again. I still loved him – I always will. Our connection runs so deep that it will always shine brightly, even after falling in love with another romantic partner. I didn't mention my new budding relationship – I knew it would break his heart.

After I waved them both off at the train station on their way to the airport, it was now my turn to come back to a silent home without the familiar sounds of child chatter and joyful laughter. I had a taste of what I had inflicted on Michael two years earlier. For a fleeting moment, I once again questioned my decision to leave. Was Michael right that I had been cowardly to give up the fight? Was I sabotaging our love - the sweetest love I had ever known?

I didn't realise it then, but that farewell to James marked what was to be the first of many separations between mother and son; and father and son, over the years to come, as we now entered a new chapter of co-parenting from opposite sides of the world.

On the positive side - and there are always positives to be found in any situation - James's absence afforded Andrew and I quality time to cement our blossoming relationship. I'd moved on from the pokey flat that my mum helped me clean up, to a much-improved apartment in the catchment area for a good local school. Soon, Andrew was spending most evenings at my place.

We were developing strong feelings, and I knew I would soon have to tell him my story before things became more serious. My dilemma was, when would be the right moment? I still hadn't decided on that 'right' moment, before he ended up moving in. He came over to mine on Christmas Day evening because he needed a break from the festive tensions of his own family Christmas, and he pretty much didn't leave after that.

I knew I had to find the courage to tell him. When I could put it off no more, I instigated a run along the beach. It was a crisp

January morning, and when we reached a beautiful spot I said, 'Let's just stop here for a rest shall we?' We sat on a wall looking out onto the still Atlantic Ocean. 'I've got something important to tell you,' I ventured.

It was the hardest thing to find the right words, but somehow, I did. He listened patiently and when I'd finished, we sat in silence as he processed what I had just disclosed.

'I am a bit shocked.' He said at last.

My heart sank. Perhaps I thought he would take it in his stride as Marcus had. But I would be kidding myself if I believed it was not an enormous thing to digest for a new romantic partner. For a moment I feared my disclosure was too much for him to cope with and I may have ruined things. But then to my relief he reached for my hand and said, 'I just need some time to process this.' We ran home in silence.

In the days that followed, we talked more about it. He made a genuine effort to understand, asking me lots of questions. In the early phase of a relationship, when you discover the first shortcomings about a new partner, the rose-tinted glasses make it difficult to walk away.

He took time to digest the news and ultimately concluded that he loved me and accepted me as I am. If that had been part of my life's journey, then it had shaped who I was now, and that was who he had fallen in love with.

Sharing it with him was a huge relief and it brought us closer because it signalled growing trust and openness between us. I was learning that Andrew was a solid, uncomplicated man and he just wanted someone to trust and accept him as he was, just as much as he was willing to trust and accept the person he chose to be with.

As you can imagine, being apart from James for the first time ever, there were lots of long-distance phone calls between Michael's household and mine either late at night or early in the morning. This could not have been easy for Andrew so soon after he moved in, but he never objected. He understood my maternal devotion to James and my need to speak with him regularly.

Before James's three-month holiday was up, Michael asked if he could have him to stay a bit longer to make the most of the freedom we had before he started school.

I resisted at first, then acquiesced that my objections were selfish ones – based on how much I would miss my little boy. This would be the only opportunity for an extended period with his daddy before starting school in the upcoming September. So again, I agreed for the same reasons as before, thinking it was in James's best interests. But oh, how it broke my heart when, a few weeks later, Michael sent me a video, filmed on his camcorder, of the pair of them on a nighttime picnic. James sat on the bonnet of Michael's car singing, '*My best Mumma's gone forever, my best Mumma's gone forever.*' There were no video calls in those days and so for months he had only heard his beloved Mumma's distant voice through a phone receiver when the time difference allowed. Unable to place her whereabouts, and having no concept of world travel, he must have just thought in his sweet young mind that I had abandoned him!

If I had for one minute predicted how this to-ing and fro-ing between countries would affect him, I never would have agreed for him to leave for so long. But the extension of James's stay with his daddy did pave the way for another significant life event that I didn't see coming.

Chapter 20
Shut Out
1998

It was now March, and the first notes of spring were gracing our seaside town. Out of the blue, Andrew suggested going for a casual dinner. 'There's this new pizza restaurant that apparently does amazing calzones.'

I was a little surprised by his suggestion because the restaurant was in the student quarters, and we normally had no reason to go there. But off we went in his car. He wasn't a chatterbox anyway, but today he seemed quieter than usual.

When we pulled up in a carpark, he said. 'When someone proposes, does it need to be somewhere romantic?'

My mind raced. 'I can't answer yes to that question, if he's about to propose,' I thought urgently. I thought fast and replied with something like, 'No I suppose not. It's however the mood takes you, I guess.'

He was quiet for a moment as he turned towards me in his seat and seemed a bit nervous. 'Ok great...well...will you marry me? 'He was smiling and looking into my eyes for a reaction.

There had been no talk of marriage in our four months of being together. We'd been intensely getting to know each other, but this proposal came totally out of the blue for me. I loved him though, and I could see no reason to say no, so I said yes!

'Let's go and have our pizza then!' He was relieved and delighted by my response, and this was exactly his style. No fuss. Loving and dependable but not overly demonstrative with his emotions.

I felt happy, loved and secure. But for some reason I didn't feel moved to elation as I had always imagined a marriage proposal would do. I kept trying to push away the intrusive thought that this is not what it would have been like with Michael. With him, there would have been poetry and electricity and moonlit evenings.... Stop it! I admonished myself for even having those kinds of thoughts. I should find joy in my new life, with this kind and gentle man, who loves and accepts me as I am.

He didn't present a ring at that point. That came a week or so later when Easter fell. Andrew presented me with a huge deluxe chocolate egg. He watched my face in amusement as I opened it to feast on the hidden goodies, and instead discovered my engagement ring snuggled inside! It was a thoughtful and lovely surprise. So, I got a little cross with myself for having a sudden memory from the past rush back during such a beautiful moment.

The memory was from Michael's visit to London after that fated ski trip in Meribel – the one where I went cold on poor Sean. Then, he had presented me with a striking ruby ring while shopping on Oxford Street. We knew we could never get married, but being the colourful, effusive character he was, he wanted to act out a mock proposal and let me know that he would marry me in an instant if we could. He'd bought the ruby during a stopover in Thailand on his first trip to England when he met Janet – the same trip when he called a friend about his alarming premonition that he was going to meet Janet again.

Then, in London, he commissioned a jeweller to make it into a ring. He had mapped out a design and handed his drawing to the jeweller. The bright jewel was to be set in the middle encased in gold threads with a small diamond on either side. He said the inspiration for the design was that the ruby represented our love in the middle, the diamonds on each side represented our souls, and the gold threads represented our individual journeys to get to each other. I had been stunned by its beauty but consumed by a heart wrenching sadness at the same time, knowing that this ring could never herald upcoming marriage to this man. I treasured and wore it for years as a reminder of our allegiance. I still have it today and it serves as a bittersweet reminder of the love that was not allowed.

The diamond on my finger now, from Andrew, was lovely - designed with tasteful simplicity but understated in comparison to Michael's flamboyant taste. I was happy to be accepting Andrew's proposal of marriage - he had an abundance of qualities that I was looking for in a partner. He was kind, honest, dependable, generous and supportive. So I was slightly troubled by the wistful memories now surfacing of Michael.

Growing up, we are conditioned to think of a marriage proposal as the pinnacle of success in a loving relationship. I suppose it was inevitable that this proposal would shine a light on the sad reality that Michael and I could never express our love and commitment through this ritual. I suppose it's normal for couples to find themselves having niggling doubts about whether they are doing the right thing in the moments after getting engaged. My only concern was whether I could truly give this wonderful man my whole heart and at last stop dwelling on the love I had walked away from.

***

When I told my parents of our engagement, they were delighted. To them this signalled that I was putting my relationship with 'that man' - as they referred to Michael - behind me. Getting engaged was the final proof that I was at last moving on and letting go. They both very much approved of Andrew, whom they found charming and saw as successful.

As a celebration, they invited us to join them in Florida while they were housesitting. Everyone who was close to me now knew my story, and so I felt I could finally be my authentic self – open and uncompromised. A normal life seemed well within reach.

The house-sit, something my parents often did in order to travel cheaply, was situated on a lake in a gated community near a swampy area where crocodiles roamed. It was incredible. I hadn't been on holiday with them for years and it felt nice now to share new experiences with them in an unfamiliar environment, not as a dependent anymore, but as an engaged independent woman. It had been a tough road for my mum since 'the confession' but I was hopeful that we could now put it behind us.

Andrew and my dad got on well. Fascinated by my dad's civil service career, Andrew enjoyed listening to his stories about assignments in different parts of the world. He, like my parents, had been brought up to feel that status and job titles were important for a sense of purpose, which led to mutual approval.

My mum was preoccupied with hating Michael at this point. She brought it up with Andrew a couple of times. I overheard them chatting and caught my mum saying something about keeping Michael out of my life. I didn't hear exactly what either of them said, but I got the tail end of Andrew's concluding comments, 'I love her, and I will be there for her. I'm totally committed to her and James.'

This was the first sign that there was some plotting to keep Michael away from me, but it would not have been appropriate for me to confront them then. Now was not the time to risk a falling out with my parents when we'd just started building bridges.

We all went fishing together and I remember a majestic heron landing on the deck right next to us. It was an exotic place with the hot sun and the incredible wildlife, and we were feeling relaxed and happy. Andrew and I would go off and do our own thing sometimes. We hired bikes and cycled along the river, and then took a few days to stay on our own in an old-fashioned guesthouse in another town on a recommendation. I remember the quaint wooden shutters. We were very much in love, although I was aware it had a different level of intensity to the all-consuming love that I had with Michael. We enjoyed getting to know each other more deeply, but I observed we didn't talk as much as I was used to with Michael. Andrew was more introverted than me - more considered in his choice of what was worth expressing in words. We found plenty of fun though.

In a happy coincidence, our trip coincided with a world-famous Harley Davidson event, which Andrew was very excited about. Bikers from all over the USA gathered in the town for the weekend and proudly rode *en masse* through the streets to show off their prized bikes to all the curious and admiring onlookers. It was quite a spectacle, and very loud!

All the bars in the area were full of leathered bikers. We went to one and ended up chatting and playing pool with a group of them. They looked so scary from afar with all their leathers and tattoos, but they were soft as pussy cats when we got talking! It felt great to connect to a new group from a different walk of life and hear about their cult hobby. I admired how free they were to express themselves with their opinions and crazy outfits.

***

Shortly after we returned to the UK that summer, James returned from Australia, now aged 4, ready to start primary school. Michael made the trip to accompany James on the plane but I refused to let Michael stay with us overnight. I told him I was in a serious relationship but stopped short of telling him I was engaged. I did not think he would be ready to stomach that news. He stayed in a hotel for one night before travelling back across the globe, the conspicuous absence of his little flight companion breaking his heart once again. He was returning home once more to grieve the loss of his day-to-day life with his beautiful son.

I had missed James terribly, and he me. Hours after a tear-jerking goodbye to his beloved daddy, he met Andrew for the first time. He was quiet and shy at first but Andrew was wonderful with him. He broke the ice by presenting him with a blue inflatable space hopper. It can't have been an easy time for James. Barely had the goodbye tears for his daddy dried, when he was introduced to a new male figure in his life. Thinking about the loss and confusion he was unable to express makes my heart ache. Being so young, he couldn't understand why he and his mummy and daddy couldn't live happily together.

I was relieved to find that despite more than six months apart, our bond was as strong as ever. He seemed to take it in his stride that he had a new stepdad. I've since learned that children always appear to adapt easily because they have no choice. The alternative is to become overwhelmed. The three of us settled into our new life together in my seaside flat. James had regular contact with his dad on the phone, which was agonisingly little consolation for Michael, who missed his son desperately with every day that passed.

Things did not stay sanguine for long, however. Now that I was engaged, my parents re-involved themselves in my life, and their grandson's. They had decided, in their wisdom, it would be better that James never saw his father again. Their hatred for Michael had been festering away ever since my confession.

My mum blamed him for everything. The only way my parents could process my story was to vilify him and victimise me. On some level, I felt relief that my mum was so stoic in her support of me. Sadly, in my selfish desire for my own survival it suited me for them to see me as the vulnerable one, not the perpetrator.

They put pressure on me to sever ties with Michael once and for all. They involved my extended family to reinforce their argument, and even tried to recruit Andrew in their opinionated campaign. Suddenly everyone seemed against the idea of Michael maintaining any relationship with his son. Everyone said he should leave us both alone. Then, my parents rang Michael's mum in Birmingham and told her the truth. From there followed an earnest phone call to two of Michael's siblings.

This marked the start of a new chapter of conflict. Unlike my family, they had no inkling that something like this was up. They were straight, professional people who lived conventional lives. This was such a shock to them.

My family arranged a meeting with Michael's brother and

sister, who held similarly strong views about the whole thing. Because Michael had moved away from his family aged 18, they had lost touch with who he was. He hadn't matured with them into their adult years, as they had done with each other. In their eyes he was the black sheep who emigrated to Australia.

It was agreed that the meeting should be at our house in Weston-super-Mare, but it was better if I went out. I went along with it. I would not have been able to cope with being present in their meeting anyway. I left them all with Andrew, discussing what was best for my life and my son's, as if I had no autonomy. The scenario had all the echoes of my childhood, when I felt like I had no say in my own choices. Maybe that's why I let it happen.

An alliance was made with my parents and Michael's siblings that it was better all-round if Michael did not see James until he was 25. Andrew declared his commitment to being the best and supportive stepdad he could be, so James would not be without a father figure. It seemed like they all wanted to pretend our relationship had never happened.

Michael's brother wrote to him in Australia. The formal address began, '*Dear Michael, we have come together as a family and have all agreed it's best that you don't see Sophia and James.*' It went on to say that he should '*do the right thing and leave them alone.*'

There was big fracas between Michael and his family. He was indignant. These people, who hardly knew him anymore, were making decisions, from another country, about whether he could see his own son! He pointed out in a series of lengthy and highly articulate letters that this beautiful little boy would grow up his whole life wondering what happened to his father when contact was so abruptly cut off. And how ridiculous it would be to introduce him to some 'eccentric grandfather' at the age of 25, and not expect him to piece it together. James would be surely crushed when he discovered all the deceit around him.

I was swept along with the whole thing – I felt powerless to do anything. At first, I kept trying to defend Michael, 'Stop! We loved each other. It was mutual!' But it was fruitless and I needed my family united around me. They had all helped me as a single mother and I didn't want to throw this back in their face with animosity. I was also delicately engaging a new stepfather figure into James's life, always conscious of giving sufficient love and attention to both my infant son and my fiancé.

I was surrounded by their strong views and sometimes I did get swayed into thinking their plan may be the right thing. I naturally wanted to please Andrew. But then again, it didn't feel right - on a soul level – for my son not to see his dad again. Whenever James was with his dad, he thrived. I saw how happy he was when he came back from Australia from his extended stay and how excitedly he told me about the adventures he and his daddy had enjoyed. I was in so much turmoil. Again.

It did not help that ever since Andrew and I met, he'd had to endure Michael calling all the time, wanting to speak to James and me. Michael and I always had lots to say to one another, and so we talked above and beyond what is normal for two exes in a co-parenting situation. With GA relationships, the abiding connection never fades!

In the beginning, Andrew was accepting that I spoke to Michael often. He had heard my raw story, told from my heart, and understood that there was nothing but integrity behind our love motives. But I was his girl now, and at best he must have felt a little irritated by the intrusion of such regular phone calls. Now that my whole family were galvanised to get Michael out of my life, it was only natural that he went along with this. It was easier for him if they had their way and Michael was out of the picture.

Michael became the scapegoat and I didn't have the conviction to stop the force of opinion. They wanted me to condemn him, like they did. I was left with little choice but to go along with their narrative. I have to admit, it was easier for me that they saw me as the victim. It let me off the hook.

The irony was not lost on me that I had felt so free with Michael, whereas now that I was back with my family, I felt all the old constraints of expression. Michael was the person who enabled me to find my authentic voice and express my individuality with confidence. Now, I was regressing back to that conformist young girl, trying to be the 'good girl', who did as she was told. My family were advocating that Michael just disappeared from my and James's life, presenting it as an opportunity to put that difficult, taboo phase behind us and start afresh.

The cacophony of disapproval around me made me occasionally question whether Michael did have some sort of pathology in pursuing his attraction for me – his daughter, 19 years his junior. In moments of emotional confusion, I accused him of ruining my life and we would have bitter rows. But he never held our heated exchanges against me. Like a father with prevailing loyalty for his daughter, he always carried on loving me, no matter how painful things were for him.

He would plead for my support to safeguard his relationship with his son, reminding me that no matter what we've been through, we are still family and need to maintain a good relationship for James' sake. The whole period was awful and I became very stressed - torn between defending the man I once had so much regard for and who was the father of my child; and launching a fruitless defence against all the people close to me.

There was one particularly awful incident where my family wrote a vitriolic letter to Michael, informing him that I had agreed not to speak to him. They told him that I had come to my senses and saw him as the irresponsible man that he was.

I wrote a sympathetic letter to Michael in response, expressing how mortified I was about the meeting at my house which had taken place without me. I clarified that, of course, I did not think like they did, but I was under so much pressure to acquiesce. Allowing them to think I had severed ties with him was purely for their benefit - so that they could get closure.

In my letter, I begged for understanding that I had to play this role. Not for my benefit, but for the healing of my family, and to save our son from witnessing more family rifts. And that I would never, ever ostracise him from my life. I would never forget our love. I would never deny him seeing his son.

Tragically, my letter got delayed.

Michael, aghast at what he perceived to be a deceitful side of me he had never seen before, taped the next one of our friendly phone calls. I was my normal, chatty self with him. Michael thought my family needed to know that I was playing double agent; That I did not hate him; That our connection was as pure, as consensual, as natural and as organic as it ever was. He sent these tapes to my family and more fights erupted.

The following is an extract from a letter Michael sent to me, after sending those tapes to my family.

> *...And that brings me to mention the tapes. I wonder if you could understand, please, and forgive me. They of course were sent before I got your long overdue letter – held up, I understand. That the conclusions of the meeting – as I then knew of them – were so one-sided, and unfair and draconian; and so reflecting of a distortion of what I've been up to, – how things had happened and been managed – and of where I was coming from; that by definition, I knew I had no way of correcting the views that were formed – the prejudices and the assumptions beneath them. I was desperate, Sophia.*
>
> *I knew that what was fairly needed was a correction of the behaviour and feelings between you and Andrew, and that meant ending cozy communications with me. But artifice and distortion was clearly being engaged to construct a wicked argument: I was the source of all evil, as your mum said; And that what James needed was to have me – in effect – marginalized, and to pull some far-off, grown-up cousins out of the hat. And that this all was good, and had some humanistic and compelling logic!*
>
> *Sophia, I was really desperate to try to modify the misunderstanding; and needed to be acknowledged as well-meaning and desirous of a happy, responsible, sane,*

caring, stable outcome. Please, please, don't be offended if I say that, perhaps the desire to please everyone, that you have been – for many reasons, not least, the pressure you've been under from your parents; and parenting; from me in the past – not really since you met Andrew and lived with him; and from your own caring concerns as a mum – you have been tragically inconsistent and very often deceitful. I was, in effect, being threatened with this not-so-thin end of the wedge, in the loss of my son.

That bond, I believe, is valid and inalienable – regardless of its origin some years ago. Please believe that I anguished endlessly about what I should do. The tapes were questionable, I know. And I hated breaking your confidence. I know now, of course, that you did play some tapes of your own to your mother, that may have been less fairly representative of how I routinely dealt with you, than mine were.

But after all, the tapes relate real factual exchanges and feelings. They obviously are judged and discounted as a questionable relevance by anyone who heard them. And I was desperate for any hearing at all.

Dear Sophia, fairly recently, you were so sincere when you said that we deserve to be allowed to have a sane and calm relationship, despite what's happened, forever. I still pray for that, and I want you to know that I still honour that; and that for me, what you expressed will always have deep meaning. I feel perhaps, I'm not doing so well with this wretched letter. That I'm going the wrong way. Of course, there's a great pressure to review your letter, paragraph by paragraph. Perhaps you'd like me to. Perhaps it's pointless, so in a minute, I'll try to end this and come to conclusions….

***

This is one of the few surviving letters I have from Michael. I am still full of regret to say that I succumbed to pressure from my mum to throw them away.

I remember it so clearly. Ahead of moving into a new home with Andrew, my mum visited to help me pack. We happened to find a big cardboard box in the attic. Inside were reams of love letters between Michael and me, some 20 pages long. There were poems, sketches, and all manner of memorabilia charting our plight over the years. It included the cartoon with the 'I hope she's not cross' caption, which he drew and sent when he first contacted me. They reflected our unique private language of love, our in-jokes, our memories.

'What's this?' My mum asked.

'They're just my letters.'

'What, love letters from Michael? You still have them!' I didn't know how to object. 'Sophia, this is your new life with Andrew now. You just got engaged. Throw them away! That era is over.'

She was so forceful, I did as I was told. Even now, at age 33, I still felt I had no choice, and together we put them in a binbag.

Michael couldn't get over it when I told him years later. 'That was *my* life too. This was *my* love too. *My* letters. You should have sent them back to me!' I lamented this impulsive act so much for months – actually, years. How could I let myself be influenced by mum like that? I woke up with hot sweats from ruminating how much this hurt Michael. We could have perhaps shown them to our son one day.

So many heartfelt letters, providing a window into how we talked, how we loved, how we were with each other. And except for just a few, they are all gone.

Chapter 21

The Long Reckoning

1998 - 2000

At some point during this period of family strife, I have a memory of going to see a psychic. I had never seen one before, but I was still on my path to understanding different forms of spirituality and was increasingly becoming fixed on the idea that we are all connected to a higher power. Frankly, I would have grasped at anything which promised clarity during this horrible time.

The name of a psychic called Tom Smith kept coming up in recommendations, so I joined the long waiting-list. When the time came, I attended my appointment with James and left him playing in the waiting area, just outside Tom's room. It transpired that this very respected spiritual guide was less interested in me, and more in James. During our session, he told me that the primary thing coming through to him was my son, who he had merely glimpsed in the waiting area. He said he had a vision of him standing amid the colours of UN flags, giving a talk on a large platform of some sort. I didn't really know what to make of it, but I'll never forget it.

Also during this tumultuous time, I remember Michael asking several times if he could visit James, and I refused. But then I would feel so remorseful that I'd change my mind and tell him on short notice that he could come. It was awful for him, I know. He couldn't plan anything. But this was the bewildered, torn, malleable state I was in. At the height of the tension, Michael engaged lawyers to ensure he retained access to James. How could our relationship have reached such a low?!

There was a family court hearing and even though the judge was told about our biological relationship - the fact that Michael was both James's grandad and dad, they discounted this fact and said there was no need to put any court order in place to stop Michael seeing James. This was all at great financial cost to Michael.

To think how we'd gone from such fervent adoration to this embittered situation. Human beings can get themselves into such a mess. I couldn't bear him suffering so much, and I beat myself up even more for not being able to stand by him. What hurt he must have felt, thinking about everyone ganging up against him, including me!

In an attempt to offer an olive branch, and to show Andrew what a good man Michael really was, I suggested we visit Australia for the New Year celebration. Michael was always alert to any opportunity to see James and had asked many times if he could visit the UK. I am sorry to say that I'd agree and then change my mind, all because I was trapped in this crazy quagmire of opinions, my voice of reason drowned out by the judgement of those around me.

My idea for a New Year visit provided an opportunity to try to put it right. Michael paid for us all to travel there. Andrew was hesitant about meeting this man, towards whom he had very mixed feelings, and whom my family had in effect poisoned him against. We stayed in Sydney, so we could welcome in 1999 while watching the world-renowned firework display off Sydney Harbour Bridge. This presented the trip more as a family holiday for us, rather than a visit to the ghosts of my past in Perth. Michael also travelled across the country to Sydney to meet us so we could all be on neutral territory.

When the two men met, they were very civil. My heart went out to both of them for being forced into such an unusual and strained situation. Michael later told me that when he met Andrew, he felt relief, because he could tell that he was a decent, reasonable man and it gave him hope that with him around to provide a voice of rationale to my parents, he could stand a chance of maintaining access to his son.

On New Year's Eve, we all went to a stunning northern beach and then to lunch in the city centre. As we tucked into delicious food, I remember feeling so proud of these two men for making efforts to understand the other. I was touched that they could sit there, being respectful to each other, both in love with me in different ways. I remember thinking, 'We can do this! We can all get on. We can amicably be involved in co-parenting. There doesn't need to be friction and division.'

That evening, Michael was planning to take James to a party at one of their friends' homes, leaving Andrew and I to enjoy an evening on our own. But when his friend announced that no other kids would be at the party, Michael decided to take James to watch the Sydney Harbour fireworks instead. He later told me that as he and James walked above the harbour, he looked down onto the crowds, knowing that somewhere in there were me and Andrew having a romantic dinner for two, and he felt a surge of loneliness.

When we returned to the UK, I felt somewhat comforted that I'd alleviated the tension with Michael and that the two men in my life had met and could hopefully now see each other as good souls. But the resentment and disapproval from my extended family was still very much there.

***

I felt mostly settled and content in my life with Andrew and James. We moved into a new and bigger home. I was still working in the same private hospital as I did when I first moved to Weston-super-Mare from Australia, and Andrew was doing well in his job. He was dependable, loyal and hardworking. I loved him very much, but I was ever conscious that our relationship had less fervour than I had experienced with Michael. How could any relationship be on a par with something so unusual and biological in nature? Andrew was aware of this too. It wasn't a smooth ride for him knowing our history and then being constantly reminded of it every time the home phone rang and stole me away for an hour or more. When we were out and about as a family, people assumed that he was James's dad, and in some way we both wished that was the case.

We kept putting off the task of planning our wedding. I just didn't have the headspace to organise it, alongside all the things that go with trying to run a smooth family life. I spent a lot of time helping James re-adjust to our new family dynamic and settle into his new school routine. This took precedent over setting a date to tie the knot.

To add to these competing priorities, Andrew and I had a motorbike accident - losing control as we skidded on a spillage of unseen diesel on the road. I shattered my right wrist into twelve pieces, which left me in hospital for over a week. As part of my reconstruction surgery, doctors had to shave some bone off my hip which they used to fuse my wrist. Andrew seemed unscathed at the time, but within a few hours developed a high temperature. He had a quinsy – an abscess of the throat, brought on by the stress of the accident so we were in quite a pickle for a while. Friends and family rallied around, but it was a frustrating time. Andrew felt dreadful, and James had to accept being looked after by anyone willing to help out.

Then, not long after my plaster came off, in the autumn of 1999, I found out I was pregnant! Severe morning sickness meant that I had to take time off work. Andrew was extremely attentive and understanding and we were excited to have another addition to our family on the way.

In June 2000, I went into premature labour and our son was born at only 4lbs 11oz. His tiny body was thankfully healthy, and with lots of skin-to-skin contact and exclusive breastfeeding he was soon thriving.

We named him Lucas, which means 'the bringer of light'. James, now aged six, adored his baby brother. I loved everything about being a new mother again, but the six-year sibling age gap was not insignificant. Andrew worked long hours and being home alone, navigating the needs of James and a premature newborn created some relationship challenges.

I started to notice that James was always trying to please Andrew. It made me extra protective of him, as I assumed this reflected how much he missed his daddy. Andrew was incredibly loving with him, but it is a whole different psychological and spiritual connection when a child is your own flesh and blood. It was as if James, on some level, recognised how much Andrew doted on the new baby and was aware that his feelings for him, while loving, were different.

Whatever the subtle dynamics were, Andrew and I tried our best to make James feel secure now that another family member had arrived. This gave me more reason to grant James some much needed time with his daddy. When Lucas was five weeks old, in July 2000, I took both boys to Australia for a month-long holiday. I hoped that this would offer a break for Andrew too, and could disperse some of the tension we had been feeling.

Off I went again to the other side of the world. Michael sorted out a rental apartment near to him and Natalie, who was by now heavily pregnant herself. Seeing how happy James was visiting his dad, I reluctantly agreed to let him stay on in Australia for a few months. I figured it would give me a chance to restore the relationship equilibrium with Andrew and have focused time with our newborn.

But when I returned to the UK, in the September, it was difficult to settle. I missed James too much, and I also found myself missing Michael, now not in a romantic way, but I missed talking to him about stuff including parenting decisions over our beloved James. While I had no fantasy of ever getting back with him, I was drawn to being near him. I missed his company; the security I always felt around him; and the joy of being able to make decisions and observations about James's development together.

It was yet again a challenging and confusing time. Andrew

and I didn't share the same depth of communication that I had with Michael, and that made it harder to understand each other's emotions. I am a big communicator – I like to analyse and articulate emotions. I think a lot. If something doesn't make sense, my reaction is to say, 'let's talk about that.' This is what enabled Michael and I to navigate our difficulties for so long. Andrew was less inclined to talk in depth. He told me that it all goes on in his head – his emotions and feelings are all there in good working order. But he had difficulty articulating them. He internalised feelings instead of verbalising them, and often said that talking a lot is overrated.

He was an intelligent conversationalist and a sympathetic listener, but our chats were not boundless. We did not talk deep into the night, exploring all angles, expressing wonderment about the synchronicities of the universe. He was busy at work and didn't fully understand what I was going through at home with a newborn. That's why some of our issues remained unresolved.

By November, I felt I'd done the wrong thing by letting James stay in Australia without me and his brother. I was anxious to be reunited. We discussed the practicalities of me staying there for an extended period. We deliberated for many weeks about this, worried that this could symbolise the end for us, and wanting to hold on to what we had. Eventually, with heavy hearts, Andrew and I reached the conclusion that I should go to Australia to answer my longing to be back with James.

Andrew was obviously feeling that things weren't right either. It was far from goodbye for good - just a break, we called it. We agreed that he would come to visit us at Christmas, and we'd assess our future from there. While we didn't outright describe it as me going there 'to live', that is what my instinct told me it was.

I didn't know how to tell my parents. They were away in America - on another house-sit so I wrote a letter telling them that by the time they got back I would be gone. I told them I loved them, and I felt, in the depths of my heart, that Perth was where my home should be. Recalling all this, I can't believe how many times I kept moving my life between countries, but it seemed the only way at the time.

When I finally arrived in Perth after the arduous flight, with which I was now so familiar, I opened my case and on top of my folded clothes was a note from Andrew face-up: 'I love you all and can't wait 'til Christmas. I'll miss you.'

He'd left several missives like this, on post-it notes, hidden between my clothes. Every time I took a pair of trousers out, a piece of yellow paper would flutter to the floor: 'Whatever we've been through, you are the best thing that ever happened to me.' Rolled up in one of Lucas's outfits was another, 'Look after our son, until I can cuddle him again.'

What a mess! Now I had separated my second son from his father, as well as the first. It was a heart-breaking reality I had to live with.

***

Michael set us up in a lovely rental house and furnished it with all the things needed to get settled - dining table, chairs, a sofa, a TV and all the white goods. He even bought a gorgeous, sumptuous mattress for the king size bed as well as providing me with a four-wheel drive vehicle to get around in. There was food in the fridge and a bottle of champagne to celebrate our arrival.

He hadn't told James that his mummy and baby brother were coming to visit. He wanted it to be a wonderful surprise. I was moved to tears when I went to meet them in a park. I saw James in the distance, pausing as he spotted us, working out if it really could be us, before he broke into a run towards us with a look of pure delight on his little face.

Natalie and I became unlikely friends, doing mother-and-baby activities together and I was impressed by her acceptance of our story. She'd even researched GA and was very supportive of our obvious bond, as well as our need to co-parent James.

We went to the local leisure centre together, put the children in the creche and did fitness classes and yoga. I went round for meals and we went to the park to watch James and her older daughter play. They got on like a house on fire. It seemed too good to be true.

I noticed that Michael and Natalie did many of the things that we used to do together – camping, hiking, driving around to find the best views, BBQs with beautiful wine. This didn't make me jealous. It just made me see what a great partner he is. Someone who is a doer and takes his beloved to see and do exciting things all over the place.

Michael seemed surprised that I'd come back. The thing he could never get his head around was how Andrew could let his own baby leave the country. Perhaps he didn't see the irony that he himself was forced into the same situation just a few years before.

Christmas soon came around and Andrew arrived for his planned five-week visit. It was so wonderful to see him and to be together again as a family of four. James was delighted to see him too. Andrew had become his 'other daddy'. It was a happy few weeks.

Andrew and I hadn't stopped loving each other despite everything, and we were still physically intimate. Once more I became tormented about whether I belonged here in Australia or back in the UK with him, and whether I wanted my engagement and our family life to continue.

When the time came for him to go back to the UK at the end of January, and we said our tearful goodbye, I was so confused and beaten up with guilt, that I decided to do something I had never done before: I sought out professional counselling.

I found a local psychotherapist. The first time I saw him, I arrived late, hot and flustered. It was a 30-minute drive across town on a scorching day. I got stuck in traffic and Lucas was in the back in his baby seat crying the whole way. Then I couldn't find a parking space.

'Come in Miss Greenwood,' he beckoned in a formal voice.

He sat upright, looking serious and forbidding; his office quiet and spotless.

I scuttled in with Lucas in a carrycase and muttered an apology for being late, using his first name.

'It's Doctor Scott,' he said with an expressionless face.

I was totally put out. In the rehabilitation centre I had worked in before Lucas came along, I was used to patients calling medical staff by their first names. Immediately I thought this was a bad idea. I didn't want to tell this uptight, frosty doctor my sensitive story. But it was too late now.

He let me talk and listened, saying nothing, just taking notes. When I'd finished, he looked me directly in the eye, his expression now full of compassion, and said, 'What a lot you've been through, Miss Greenwood.' It took a few sessions for him to absorb my full story. When everything was out in the open, he told me that I was one of the 'most remarkable and strong women he'd seen to have come through so much'. He asked to meet Michael for a session, who gladly agreed.

He concluded that I was probably experiencing post-natal depression after a premature birth, compounded by the stressful events over the past few years, which would have depleted my system considerably. He observed that I suffered overwhelm, not helped by the mix of hormones flooding my body after birth. He prescribed antidepressants which would work as a mood stabilizer. 'You are a strong and intelligent lady. My advice to you is to go back to England and repair things with your parents, build bridges with your devoted partner, and establish stability for you and your two children.'

He also told me how different he now saw me compared to the impression of the startled creature rushing into his office a few weeks earlier. In our first flustered session, I apparently had a tear in my trousers, and my knickers were sticking out. He must have thought, 'I've got a lively one here!'

I was also given an anti-epileptic drug with my prescription, which was supposed to complement the anti-depressants. I was still breastfeeding, so I didn't like the idea of passing the medication on in my milk. But my therapist pointed out that there was very low risk. I acquiesced and followed his recommendation.

Thanks to those sessions, and perhaps the medication, I gained the first true sense of clarity on my situation in years. I also followed his recommendation to return to the UK and devote myself to stability. This was an opportunity to honour my promise to Andrew that I would come back for Lucas's first birthday in June. I would not pitch this as a visit, but as me returning permanently.

Chapter 22
An Uncontrolled Revelation
2001 – 2003

Although I now had clear intent, it still wasn't easy to uproot again. Another gruelling long-haul flight; another packing ordeal – not knowing which belongings to keep or leave (I ended up shipping over the amazing mattress that Michael bought!); more explanations to friends; more addresses to change.

Nevertheless, I made sure I was back in time for Lucas's first birthday, so that Andrew could be part of it. James was now 7. It would be naïve to believe we could slip seamlessly back into being a family of four. Andrew was in favour of me finding my own place, but suggested we stay with him initially until I found somewhere. But then, as we settled in – between the same cosy four walls that I had left behind - we did find ourselves slipping back into our natural relationship dynamic. We were still intimate and hadn't stopped loving each other. Soon he didn't want me to leave.

On reflection, we should have had some relationship therapy so we could fully understand what we loved about, and needed from, the other. But it wasn't so common then and naval gazing was not the sort of thing that Andrew would embrace. We just plodded on, trying to patch things up, never really addressing the core issues which led to me moving away from him in the first place.

I remained on the antidepressants for six months. When I was first prescribed them, I was hesitant because I had heard that this family of drugs mute emotions and numb you. But now I understand more about them, I know that they help people navigate difficult times because they support emotional regulation and decrease the likelihood of overwhelm. The aim of these medications is to reduce emotional distress for a short period. They are not meant as a long-term solution in isolation. They are an adjunct to go with other supports in life – like friends and our living environment.

The experience gave me a newfound commitment to look after my physical and mental health. It gave me agency to take control, and when I came off the tablets, I focused on healthful and natural ways to boost my mood and improve my sense of wellbeing: Yoga, meditation, fitness, whole foods and supplements. Establishing a healthy and wholesome lifestyle became a priority.

I tried to explore Andrew's sentiments about our relationship a bit more. But he didn't see the need for deep analysis. His attitude was, 'Why do we need to talk about everything? Can't we just get on with things. I love you, and you love me.'

He was a stoic, pragmatic and conscientious man, who always looked on the bright side. I never doubted his commitment to me. He was content with what he had. It was me who had a longing for more. I started to question whether I could be satisfied with this simplicity for the rest of my life. We had good income; he was stable, steady, reliable and devoted; we had a healthy sex life. But I'd think, 'Speak to me. Tell me how you're really feeling?' Michael, on the other hand, was always right with me in mind, body and spirit. I always knew what he was thinking and feeling. He was always teaching me things.

When Andrew and I did get talking, he was so lovely and eloquent and made so much sense. I did love him so very much. I appreciated how decent he was, with such a big heart. But try as we did to rekindle our relationship, we just couldn't find the spark. After a year, just before Lucas turned two, and James was eight, we conceded that we lacked the compatibility to share and understand each other's needs. I moved out with both boys, remaining in the same area, and began life as a single parent once more.

This wasn't the end for us though. Andrew remained a wonderful dad to both James and Lucas, and a loving, supportive friend in my life. Like many relationships on the way out, we had a few more attempts. We tried, and tried, to get back together no less than four times. Each time, we eventually reached the same sad conclusion. We were just different people and had a different love language.

When I reflect, I see that all he wanted was a straightforward woman who just loved him for who he was. The difficulty was perhaps, that his way of expressing love contrasted with Michael, who saw only the best in me and made me feel like a princess. It wasn't Andrew's fault; we had different needs formed through our childhood losses and adult challenges.

Another factor is that over the years, I had developed spiritually. I had become more interested in ancient and mystical wisdom, and open to the existence of what many in the spiritual world call a Divine or Source intelligence. For me, the reason we're here in human form on planet earth is to learn and grow from our experiences and choices and to advance spiritually. I want in a partner someone with whom I can discuss the things which move me. Some people just accept the material world as it is. They get all they need from what meets the eye. There is nothing wrong with that, but in my life partner, I wish to be able to explore ideas around our higher purpose as beings in this complex but interconnected universe, and our individual evolution as people, to love and express our true selves.

One learns expression and passion by seeing it around them. Andrew, like me, had a childhood where he could not express himself freely after the loss of a parent. I feel lucky that I found the desire to awaken myself and become more expressive and curious. I now needed someone who had trodden, or was willing to tread, a similar path with me. If Andrew were to have some sort of awakening that enabled him to explore the deeper side of life, I believe we may be together now.

***

When James turned nine, around a year after I had been living alone with the two boys, my parents started voicing concerns about whether, when and how I would tell James, who was both my son and my half-brother - they were keen to point out - the truth. One day my dad said, 'If you like, I'll come over and we'll tell him together.' I was blown away because he was not by nature a deep and meaningful kind of guy, and we haven't had a close or easy relationship.

I went along with it because James had to know at some point, and nine seemed a good age. James was very mature, and I reasoned that he was too young for it to jolt him into going off the rails as it may have done if I'd waited until he was a teenager. Even by ten years old, childhood innocence can start to taper off, and if we waited for him to reach double digits, he may question why he hadn't been told sooner. Disclosing his history now, before he developed strong adolescent opinions, would give him time to accept it as his story. I had always known that I was adopted (or 'chosen' as my parents put it) and so, growing up with this knowledge meant I had accepted it into the fabric of who I am. I hoped the same would apply for James.

In retrospect, given how much my parents hated Michael, I should have seen that their motives for initiating the big reveal were not aligned with mine. They wanted control of the messaging. I didn't really think it through. It should have been me and Andrew who told him, but we were no longer living together, and I just went along with my parents' suggestion.

My dad came over to my house and said to James, 'We've got something to tell you. It's about mummy and daddy.' Then I had no choice but to follow through with the information, in the gentlest way I could think how. But my dad kept peppering it with a disapproving tone. He told James that his father was 'a bad man'. He pointed out that his mum is also his sister; his dad is also his grandad.

I was horrified and tried to play it down. But like always, whenever I was with my parents, I felt powerless to fight against them – brainwashed almost. James kept defending his daddy and questioning his grandad's logic, 'But I love my daddy and he's good to me.' My dad said something about how this should never have been. And that James has a stepdad now, who loves him just as much as a real daddy.

I had to tell Michael that I'd told James the truth of his beginnings, because James was bound to mention it in their phone calls. Michael was understandably rattled that I'd told him without consulting him on it. He thought nine years old was way too young to process and understand the complexities which led to our unusual relationship. I will never know if telling him at such a tender age was the right or wrong timing. He seemed to accept the news and has never struggled with his identity since. It was never going to be ideal timing. I trusted my intuition that the time was as right as it would ever be.

Distraught once more at how I had been led to betray Michael beyond my true nature, I allowed him to come and visit. I knew it wasn't fair for James to become influenced by all the negative things he heard. But Andrew did not approve that I'd agreed a visit. Bear in mind that when I returned from Australia to rebuild things, on the advice of the psychiatrist, I had assured Andrew that my life in Australia was over – that I was devoted to my family's stability here. 'Is he putting pressure on you again? Can't he let you get on with your life?' he asserted when he learned of the visit.

When Michael arrived, he called from the airport, right in the middle of a heated moment between Andrew and me over this exact issue. I didn't want to answer the phone at such a crucial point. Michael called and called and eventually I picked up. Andrew, now triggered, grabbed the phone from me and told Michael that if he ever stepped foot in Weston-super-Mare, he would go straight to the police station and report him for incest.

I tried to reason with Andrew, but it was no good. By now he had such antipathy towards Michael that all of the tolerance he had felt on our New Year meeting had all but dissipated.

Michael stayed in London for ten days and did not see his son. He had to cancel a ski trip he had booked for the two of them, not only losing a lot of money but then facing the return to Australia alone. After initial outrage, he then reconciled that this was part and parcel of the fallout of our difficult story. He would have to take it on the chin, without recourse, to honour the commitment he'd made to himself to support James and me – whatever that commitment unfurled.

Michael later told me that he made a conscious decision to set aside all previously assumed expectations for happiness in his own life. Hence forward, his dedicated mission was to ensure - as best as he could - the safety, health and happiness of James and me. He fully accepted that the depth of that commitment would be questioned by people and events. Nevertheless, he would do what it took because all he had left in life was to honour that commitment - to do the right thing as the gentleman he knew himself to be.

I'm sure it seems shocking that I let him cancel his holiday and return home without even seeing James. I still live with this guilt of betrayal. Even though I could understand my family's view that Michael should have stopped our relationship as the more mature adult, I also knew that their view was without illumination on the dynamics of GA. On top of that, the love Michael had for his son was like any other father's. That's why I wish I had been assertive enough to override their directives.

All I can say is that I didn't know what to do, nor who to defend. I was in the terrible space between a rock and a hard place. I was immobilised with anxiety, unable to take a stance in all the nastiness and tension around me.

Chapter 23

Accused

2003 - 2004

Not long after breaking the big news to James with my dad, the most testing trial of co-parenting presented itself. Much to the disquiet of my family, I'd let James go to visit his daddy in Australia. He had begged constantly to see him, and our old house and his favourite parks and beaches. While I may not have always had the strength to defend Michael's reputation, I did eventually always return to the principle that my son should not miss out on spending time with his dad. My family had no legal basis to stop me, and while my mum would always express her disdain at every one of James's visits to Australia, ultimately it was my decision, and I could roll with the punches.

He celebrated his tenth birthday on this visit and soon after, he dropped a bombshell: Could he stay and live with his daddy? For good!

I was mortified by the idea of James moving away at first, but Michael encouraged it, telling me how happy and fulfilled James was when he was there. I believed him because I had seen the evidence for myself. Every time James returned from his Australian roots, he looked radiant. I was torn, wanting to acknowledge and honour my son's choice, but knowing that his emigrating permanently would leave me bereft.

I will never know whether the timing of this request had anything to do with the conflicts at home and the unsettling words from his grandad about his dad being a bad man. But I do know that it was etched in his little memory because later, Michael told me that James recalled his version of the event with precision. 'Daddy,' he apparently said. 'I tried to argue with them, I told them it doesn't matter. He's my daddy and I love him. But every time I told them that, they had more bad things to say. I'm so sorry daddy, I didn't know what to say!'

Michael suggested that we seek professional advice and have James assessed by a child psychologist for signs of anxiety over all the family fighting. I agreed and we went to a centre in London specialising in counselling for families involved in adoption. It was expensive but we wanted access to experts who were aware of the complexities of Genetic Attraction relationships. The caseworkers assigned knew about our biological relationship. We hoped the process would help us be clear on where James should live, as well as checking that his hitherto unsettled childhood had not affected him.

James and I were both interviewed extensively in separate rooms and eagerly awaited the professional opinion. To my delight, the report recommended that James should stay with me. It noted that for a ten-year-old, he was more mature than expected, but he was also conflicted and experiencing mild anxiety by trying to keep both parents happy, while not fully understanding the circumstances. As adults, we shouldn't give him choice of where to live but act decisively on what we think is best. Their view was that he should stay with his mother and extended family and continue visiting his dad regularly.

When we told James, he didn't accept it. 'The people have got it wrong mummy,' he pleaded. 'I want to live with daddy,' It seemed his fragile heart knew what it wanted.

Ultimately, I had to let him go. I had had him with me for the better part of his short life so far. It felt right that his dad, who had lost so much, and had been treated so badly, could have this wish, which aligned with James's. So, I resisted the deepest desires of my own heart and let my son go.

We waited until the end of the school year before his big

move. I fretted about telling Andrew my decision. I broke it to him when we were alone, out on a boat. He was mortified as he loved James, and felt he'd been sidelined. Didn't he have a say in such a big decision as James's stepdad? I felt terrible because I knew I should have discussed it with him. But equally, I knew I had to make this far-reaching decision for James's sake, and Andrew would likely have persuaded me to keep James here. As much as I wanted that too, my inner voice told me it was the right thing for James to go.

James was excited. I don't think he realised the finality of this move, and that it would mean not seeing his little brother, nor us for an indefinable amount of time. Fortuitously, someone we knew was flying to Perth at the same time, so they chaperoned James.

I drove him to the airport, and Lucas, who was now four, cried his eyes out as his brother disappeared behind those departure gates, which held so many painful memories for me too from years past. I remember going into a shop at the terminal to buy him a teddy to try to cheer him up, fighting back my own tears so I would not stress him further.

Oh the desolation of returning to an empty house with just Lucas! But I had to carry on. I consoled myself that James would be getting more of what he needed. I knew he craved the male presence of his dad. This move also gave me a reprieve to focus on my bond with Lucas, and of course, myself.

I had made my bed; I had to ride the consequences and not let it affect my second son. I still have a Christmas card, written when James was ten, a couple of months after he moved. It reads:

> *Dear Mummy, I have missed you so much and always find it hard to be separated. I am sorry for the belated nature of this card but the thought behind it is as loving as always. You passed being a mum with flying colours!*
>
> *Can't wait to spend time with you, merry Christmas from your loving son. Xxx*

By now, Michael and Natalie had separated due to irreconcilable differences and he had a new girlfriend. Just a few weeks after James arrived, he got engaged to his new partner. Unbeknown to Michael, this triggered a whole new level of drama which went on to trouble him for many years to come.

Natalie was, by Michael's account, a scorned ex. She had keenly pushed for marriage, but Michael never felt comfortable with that. When she learned on the grapevine that Michael was engaged to someone else, it must have been too much for her because she went on the warpath.

She fabricated the worst kind of story one can about one's ex and father of a child – that Michael had abused their four-year-old son (James's half-brother, who he spent a lot of time with).

The first Micheal heard of it was when two police officers turned up at his door. He was detained and interviewed by officers and social services.

Shortly afterwards, the principal of James's school, a prestigious grammar, called Michael to tell him the police had arrived and wanted to interview James. He consented and plain clothes officers entered his classroom in the middle of a lesson and extracted him. They then interviewed him for an hour.

Thankfully James, although nervous of these towering men, spoke of his daddy with enthusiasm and love. Afterwards, the teacher rang Michael to say that the senior police officer of the two reported to her afterwards and said, 'I've met all kinds of people in this profession, and I've just interviewed the finest young man I've ever met on the job. What a wonderful young man he is. You won't be hearing any more from us.'

It didn't take the police long to deduce that Natalie's account of events did not add up and they took no further action. But she was relentless. She kept returning to the police with new stories. Eventually they told her they were dropping the case, but she could report it to an alternative independent body which oversaw welfare of children if she so wished, which she did.

This was a funded body, which provided counselling to anyone reporting a grievance against an offending parent. Despite the complete absence of any evidence other than the mother's complaint, Michael was ordered to have absolutely no contact with his child while the claims were disseminated. A condition which was as shocking as it was heartbreaking for him.

I heard about all this through my phone calls with Michael. What I retell here is from his personal recollections. When he first told me about James being interviewed in the middle of class, he was calm and matter of fact. He was never one to catastrophise, always capable of dealing with life's many and varied obstacles without burdening others.

I was shocked because Natalie and I had developed a friendship of sorts. It was true that I had seen an erratic side to her behaviour over the last year. After they split up, she had called me a few times and vented about Michael. I recall her once saying, 'You are lucky to be on the other side of the world and not have to deal with him!' I had distanced myself after that, not wanting to be a part of any more conflict. But I never imagined she would be capable of this.

What ensued from here was a stressful, hurtful and costly campaign, lasting more than a year, to slander Michael's name and keep him away from their son. It involved several family court hearings. In one of these hearings, a phone recording was played of Michael's ex screaming at Michael, while clearly holding their son in her arms. Commenting on this recording, the case supervisor, who had been assigned to spend time with the boy in the presence of both parents, told the court: 'How can any little boy hope to have a relationship with his father, when every time I go to the door of the mother's home, she exudes contempt in front of her boy towards his father. Every single time. So much so that I feel sick to my stomach.'

The case was thrown out and Natalie got a ticking off from the judge for wasting police time. An injunction was granted so that no media could report on this unfair accusation.

The ordeal left scars for all involved. Michael was devastated on so many levels – the malice from a woman he'd had a child with; the shock it had inflicted on James, who had already gone through so much; the brush with moral and legal judgment in court; and a reminder of the consequences of exposure should the nature of our relationship ever be openly revealed.

During this horrible ordeal, James started making noises about returning to the UK. He said he was desperately missing me and Lucas. But no doubt, the palpable tension played a part. It pained me to see how torn he was yet again between his two geographical lives. What hard decisions he had to endure in his short life!

Natalie, meanwhile, was still plotting. It was soon clear that she was prepared to use any means necessary to satisfy her burning desire for revenge. It was only a matter of time before she pulled her trump card – disclosing our biological relationship to authorities.

Michael found out about this when Australian police knocked on his door at 5am one morning and arrested him for 'technical incest.' When he asked what the difference is between incest and technical incest, he got no answer. He got lawyers involved and there ensued the next instalment of a lengthy, expensive battle to clear his name.

I was alerted to this fresh drama when I received a phone call on my landline back in the UK.

'Hello, this is the police. We've been asked by the Australian authorities to talk to you about a matter pertaining to events in Australia. Can you come in to speak to us on Tuesday?'

My stomach flipped. This was my greatest fear realised!

Chapter 24

The Trial

2004 - 2008

I called Michael immediately and he got onto his lawyer, who advised him to relay to me that I should say 'no comment' to everything. Absolutely everything. It was a good job they did because given how much of a believer I am in the value of open, honest conversation as an elixir to any conflict, I would have told them everything!

I put on my smartest outfit and headed to the local police station. Three burly, six-foot-something plain-clothed officers appeared and directed me into an interview room. There, they surrounded me.

Immediately I could sense that they were disarmed by me. I imagine they had read the word 'incest' and were expecting some hermit, who had been coerced and kept locked up in a room her whole life.

'Did you have a relationship with your father?' And so it began.

I smiled sweetly, looked directly into the questioning officer's eyes and said with a little hint of apology, 'No comment.'

I kept this up throughout the whole interview, maintaining equal eye contact with each of them and holding my wry smile. To every question, I replied in a gentle voice, 'No comment.'

This went on for an hour until one of them said, 'Clearly, you're not going to answer any of our questions Miss Greenwood, so we'll end this interview here. Thank you for your co-operation. We'll be in touch.' A bit of good old English sarcasm.

He stopped the tape and with a friendly eye roll waved me out of the room, confirming that I was free to go. 'Bye then,' I muttered and off I went.

I didn't hear anything for weeks and I thought this may be the end of it. Then I got another call and I recognised the voice as one of the officers from the interview. 'We've been asked by the Australian authorities to invite you in to do a DNA test.' There was a pause as I didn't know what to say. Then he resumed, 'We're asking you because they have asked us to. But from our point of view, you are not obliged to do this. It is not in the public interest for us to pursue this on our end.'

I didn't know if I was understanding correctly. Was he indirectly helping me? Again I was silent, and as if reading my mind he spelled it out, 'So if you don't want to do the DNA test, you don't have to. But we told them we would ask you.'

'Well I'd like to decline then.' I said, which he acknowledged, before wishing me well and hanging up.

That was the last time I heard from them. I could hardly believe it – my worst nightmare from the last decade had materialised and dissipated in the space of a few weeks. All that turmoil. All that fear of discovery. All that running away. And it seemed I had nothing to fear – at least not here in the UK.

But I was far from cavalier. I still felt like a criminal. And those around me did not get off so lightly. My parents also received a visit from the police, who interviewed them in their home for three hours. The experience led my 76-year-old mum to her GP again with anxiety.

Meanwhile in Australia, Michael was defending himself against real charges of incest – an ordeal that stretched on for years. Our story was so unusual there was no clear category in which to put it. Not only was his freedom at stake, but his reputation and livelihood. As an entrepreneur, character integrity is essential for winning business, especially since his clients were private individuals, rather than businesses. If he were exposed, he could lose everything.

Forming part of his defence, were no less than twenty letters of character recommendations from colleagues, clients and friends, many of them highflyers. Their generous words of support had apparently amazed his lawyers.

I was also asked to provide a letter affirming that our relationship was consensual. All the usual pressure from my adoptive family was applied, discouraging me to comply, and I'm ashamed to say I delayed his request. But I did in the end provide my letter, which was significant in his case.

He was interviewed exhaustively in three separate consultations by an internationally renowned ethicist. The conclusion presented to the court was that he found no criminality at the core of our relationship. He wrote a personal letter to Michael after the case, which reads thus:

> *Well Michael, it may help you and Sophia, if I make it clear that no ethicist that I know of would find fault in the relationship you have both had. I have found no elements of psychopathology in this process of examination, in which I was called upon to vet your ethics and your morals.*
>
> *This was a sincere and moving account of a loving and most conspicuously non-abusive relationship, formed in extraordinary circumstances, which psychologists in adoption currently understand could happen to anyone. I have no problem, as an ethicist, in endorsing your affair as devoid of criminality.*
>
> *The problem you face is that, in the jurisdiction under which you are judged, although not in many others, you will inevitably be found to have broken the law of the land. I wish you well and I sincerely wish the best for both of you, and for your son.*

Despite all this support, things did not look good for Michael's prospects. Just days before the ruling, he showed his lawyers some new academic articles about Genetic Sexual Attraction. He asked his lawyers to include them in his defence as further evidence of the grip that this uncontrollable phenomenon has on all who are affected by it. But the legal team advised against including it. They reasoned that it could rile the judge and signal that he had no remorse. Michael pointed out a very well-known case in south Australia which had recently hit headlines. The case was of a biological father and daughter called Jenny and John Deaves, who had been reunited when Jenny was 31. She had not seen her father since she was a baby when he left the family unit. Their connection was so strong they had both left their spouses, moved together to South Australia and bore two children, one of whom died within days from genetic complications.

They were charged by police for incest. However, a judge acknowledged that their relationship was a 'mutually consensual union' and ruled that they could still see each other but that they should be placed on a good behaviour order which banned them from having sex because of the risk of congenital defects of any resulting children.

It seemed ridiculous to ban someone from having sex – how can you ever police that?! But nevertheless, it set a precedent that this judge acknowledged the crucial factor of 'consent', which distinguishes GA from the darker definition of incest. The judge said their case was not typical because the pair were 'virtually strangers' when their relationship commenced.[1]

The pair had become well-known defenders of GA, speaking out on Australian national television about the incongruity of the comparison with incest. 'It was an instant attraction. There was a wow factor.... It just seemed so right and it wasn't until a month later that we realised the consequences of what this relationship was...It was never really a choice. The relationship just progressed.' Jenny Deaves defended in an interview two years later.[2]

But Michael's lawyers told him he should not compare his

---

1 The Times, April 07 2008

2 Incest: The Last Taboo, Current TV, 2010

case with this high profile one. This was a different jurisdiction and therefore set no precedent where he was. Michael went berserk. He rarely lost his temper, but this was one justified occasion.

He told them, 'I'm your client – you do as I say. You will put this evidence in my case.' They relented and inserted the new information on GA on the very eve of the conclusive court hearing which would deliver a verdict.

He was found guilty and dished a one-year suspended sentence.

Outlining his ruling, the judge addressed Michael by his full name. (This is not a verbatim quote but based on Michael's recollection): 'If I hadn't received this last-minute information, I had intended to give you a custodial sentence. I confess I don't understand all of the medical facts, but I get the sense there is a deeper backstory here and you have been victim to forces beyond your control.'

When the time finally came to leave court, Michael knew there would be waiting media. So far, they had not been able to report anything because of danger in prejudicing the case. Michael knew that now the verdict was out, there would be waiting cameras – from both national and local news. He also knew that without a mugshot of a sheepish defendant leaving court, there could be no headline story.

His lawyers offered to accompany him out of court, as is usual practice. But he was prepared for this. He politely declined, excusing himself by using the gents assuring them he would make his own way out. He then cunningly slipped into the bathrooms on a different floor, in case they came looking for him. There he waited for two hours, biding his time by reading a newspaper. He put on a moustache – prepacked with foresight in his bag - and changed into a scruffy hoodie to disguise himself. Eventually he dared emerge and asked a cleaner, who he judged to have no stake in the game, if there were any cameras outside. When they affirmed with a negative, he quietly left.

As he swiftly marched out of the court premises, he did not

dare to look around for any remaining waiting reporters. He kept saying to himself, 'don't turn around, don't turn around.' On he walked, head down, until he knew he was safe.

His efforts worked. His story, without a picture only made it into the short news summaries. There were no grand lurid headlines.

***

There were consequences for me too after his guilty verdict, and it was my parents who discovered them. They were sent the court documents from Michael's case and among them, buried in the small print, was a mention of my culpability. Because I too had broken the law, being the other half of this relationship, a warrant had been issued for my arrest should I ever return to Australia. I could not believe this was true. Surely I would have been notified?

I chose to bury my head in the sand about this for a long time. But soon enough, I wanted to visit James, so I braced myself to make some phone calls to check if this could really be true. I somehow found a number for the central police service in Australia and rang them. Nervously, I gave my name and date of birth. Then I asked, with great trepidation, if there was an arrest warrant issued for me in their system. This would be the moment of truth that I had avoided for years.

There was some tapping of keys while the official looked me up. It was as if I were inquiring about a hotel reservation! Sure enough, he confirmed that yes indeed there was a warrant attached to my file. I took a breath and asked for clarification.

'Does this mean if I ever come to Australia to see my family, I'd get arrested on arrival?'

'Madam, if you're an Australian citizen, you will always be allowed entry, but if you encounter law enforcement officers, you may be detained for questioning.' The calm voice replied.

I just about managed to thank the voice before hanging up and letting my tears flow. The thought that I couldn't return to the country that I considered to be my second home was an alarming confirmation of my predicament. The thought of someone sitting in a room and judging me – us – without any understanding of the nature of our post-adoption relationship, lumping it with incest, which is usually associated with child abuse, was deeply upsetting.

While this outcome could have been so much more devastating for both of us, the emotional, professional and physical fallout from this nasty legal ordeal still ran deep, particularly for Michael. While he served his one-year suspended sentence, he lost the edge on his business. He became paranoid that people would know about his criminal record. He later told me that every time a prospective client went quiet or picked another architect over him, he became convinced that they had heard a rumour about his court hearings. He was jumpy around his colleagues and friends. I suspect Michael suffered a form of depression after the verdict, but he may not even have known this himself. His business suffered. The vibrant, friendly atmosphere which once pervaded his office became stale and tense, and two of his best architects left for different jobs.

Yet still, throughout all this, he never blamed me. He never expressed regret for the love we shared. He still showed devotion to his sons and always tried to be positive for them and for me.

If I look back on how I ran away so many times from him; how I sometimes withheld my permission for him to see his son; how I let my family treat him, it is remarkable that he never stopped loving me. In any other scenario, an ex would be spurned if they were on the receiving end of behaviour like that. This indicated to me that our devotion was an unusual hybrid encompassing both the powerful romantic love felt by soul mates *and* the potency of shared biology. As a parent never turns their back on a child no matter how challenging their behaviour is, I sensed Michael would stay by my side regardless of the cost.

This complex dynamic underpinning the depth of our abiding love is, even to this day, not easy for us to understand or reconcile.

Chapter 25
Destiny's Plan
2008 - 2025

In the years after Michael's court hearings, I can say with relief that my life stabilised somewhat and I began to feel liberated for the first time in three decades. James lived mostly with me and Lucas during all of Michael's legal battles. In my box of memorabilia, I recently uncovered a Mother's Day card he gave to me in 2006 when he was 12 (quoted with grammatical errors gloriously intact), which offers a glimpse into our contemporaneous relationship.

> *Dear mum*
>
> *All my life since I was even in your tummy you have looked after me the best you could. There aren't many chances I get to try and repay you but mother's day is one of the rare times I do.*
>
> *Thanks for everything mum my angel, my friend, my protector and all those other wonderful things you are to me. I hope you enjoy today because you haven't been the last few weeks. I want you to know that I am always grateful and I think your great mama.*
>
> *Love from James xxxxoooo*

Two years after this card was written, in 2008 when he was 14, he moved back again to Australia to live. He wasn't enjoying secondary school in the UK and his dad offered him the opportunity to go to a prestigious school in Perth. I knew it was important for him as a developing young man to experience his fatherly influence, so when he expressed a desire to go, I encouraged it, although it broke my heart to see him leave again. He's pretty much lived there ever since, except for a year in his early 20s when he came back to live with Lucas and I, to test if he could settle back in England. He stayed for a year but concluded that it was a better way of life in Perth. I was devastated once more, but I understood. He had wonderful friends there and the outdoor lifestyle suited him.

A significant milestone to my emotional freedom came in 2013, shortly after Lucas turned 13 and James was 19. I felt it was time to tell Lucas the truth about his brother's father. He was blissfully unaware, but his heartwarming reaction enabled the final curtain of closure for me.

Unlike the unfortunate scenario where I made the big reveal to James, I made sure that I told Lucas when we were alone and comfortable at home - free from anyone else's ulterior motive this time. When I dropped this no-doubt alarming news, his eyes welled up and he hugged me tight.

'Oh mum! What you've been through! It's over now. It's over.' He comforted. The emotional intelligence of my two boys continues to blow me away. Then he added, 'Let's call Michael and James now, and tell them I know. We can all talk about this from now on openly.' Which we did, and there were many tears of relief.

The next day we invited Andrew round to tell him that the big family secret, which had preoccupied me for more than half of my life, was now in the open. The three of us shared one of the most honest and emotional conversations we'd ever had. Lucas's reaction was the ultimate acceptance. There was nothing left in the closet now. No more consequences to fear. Except, of course, for that warrant for my arrest should I ever return to Australia.

***

Another loose end I was able to reconcile, which as a reader you may find heartening, is the opportunity to explain to Sean why I went so mysteriously quiet on him after that ski trip.

This came sometime in the summer of 2015. I had started to take on modelling and minor acting jobs, which I continue to enjoy today, and which has been a liberating creative outlet for me. A casting came up near the South Bank in central London. A few months earlier, I had made a prayer, directed to my guardian angel, asking for the opportunity to clear any unresolved issues arising from incidents where I may have inadvertently hurt anyone in my life, or they me. What happened next blew my mind because it seemed like a direct answer to this plea of my heart.

After the casting, I asked an acquaintance, who I had got to know from similar jobs on the circuit, if he'd like to go for coffee. He regretted that he didn't have time but suggested we walk together to the Tube. We passed a table on the pavement outside a café on which a beam of sunshine had managed to find its way between buildings. It seemed to be beckoning us to sit down. 'Oh, go on then, I have 15 minutes,' he said, and we settled ourselves at the little table. It was rush-hour and all the commuters around the busy London Bridge area came pouring out - hundreds of mostly white men in dark suits carrying briefcases. We joked that we felt like extras in *The Thomas Crown Affair*!

Before we got a chance to delve into any quality conversation, my eyes were drawn to a man briskly walking past. He wore sunglasses but I recognised his mouth. I knew, in my whole being that it was Sean! I jumped up and squawked to my acquaintance, 'Watch my bag for a minute!' and I disappeared into the sea of suits. I dodged through the crowds, trying to catch sight of him again in the thronging sea of suits. Eventually I saw him as I looked down a side street and rushed to catch up. I tapped him on the shoulder. 'Sean?'

I now had long hair and was some 25 years older than the

pixie-cut twenty-something he had once dated. He turned around. 'Yeah?'

'It's Sophia.'

'Sophia? Oh my god. We were just talking about you last week!'

We stared at each other. He said he was en route to meet someone at a nearby pub and invited me to join. I nipped back to the guy who'd been very good-humouredly guarding my abandoned bag, while he missed his train! I apologised profusely, explaining that I'd met an old friend, and accompanied Sean to the pub.

There, I got my opportunity to say, 'I'm really sorry,' and I revealed my story. He didn't directly inform me, but I could tell he already knew. He gave me a hug and told me it was ok. He was happily married now with three boys. We took a selfie and sent it to the two others who were on that ski holiday with us. When his friend arrived in the pub, Sean introduced me. Without a blink, his friend said: 'Sophia? You mean the Sophia who broke your heart in France?'

I had a flash then that this could have been my life. I could have had three children with him, lived in a big house in the home counties and not encountered any of the strife and pain that has run through my life. I didn't really give him a chance, did I? But then I remembered, that could never have happened because GA relationships are – by their very nature - almost unstoppable once they take hold.

***

The last decade has been the calmest of my life. It has allowed me to reflect with an open heart on how much mine and Michael's lives were influenced by this little-understood force of nature that is known as Genetic Attraction (or Genetic Sexual Attraction, as official literature calls it), and how our lives and those around us were changed irrevocably by our forbidden love.

For two decades, I carried a secret, only disclosed to a select few. I guarded this secret because all my decisions were made from a place of fear. I read a book during this reflective period called, *Feel The Fear And Do It Anyway* by Susan Jeffers. It resonated with me because it highlighted the insidious power of fear-based thoughts. It suggests that if we face what we are afraid of, fears dissipate because they are just illusions of the mind. I now feel, at last, that I have the courage to speak up.

Another helpful phrase for me came in a book called *Everyday Wisdom* by one of my favourite authors, Wayne Dyer. He said: 'Whatever the question, love is always the answer.' I try to follow this philosophy. If we follow our hearts, with trust and good intention, there is nothing to fear, only fear itself. The positive energy of love is what liberates us and empowers us and is our greatest healer. We should always look at how we can offer love instead of reacting to our inner fears.

You'll recall that I've always been open to spiritual ideas about who we are and why we're here; and that over the years I've searched for answers about the nature of reality and why we experience what we do. I've now come to firmly believe, as many great spiritual writers and teachers over the centuries have proposed, that there is a higher intelligence at play – not connected to any specific religion – but an all-knowing, loving and infinite organising intelligence to the universe and that there is only perfection. Everything is as it should be. There are no mistakes. It's not what happens to us, but how we perceive it and what we do with it, that shapes our reality of it.

This understanding has enabled me to come to terms with our story: It feels like we were always destined to meet. Michael and I would have eventually felt compelled to find each other. Having done so, despite the pain we have endured, we don't wish we hadn't!

Whatever crucible our destinies were forged in, it felt like an unbreakable alloy, illuminated by the sparks that fly when the tangled wires of genetic attraction connect. For me, our unexpected and unusual experience of deep and unconditional love was like a spiritually guided journey. It reminds me of an excerpt in a book called *The Prophet* by the poet, artist and philosopher, Kahlil Gibran in the late 1800s:

> *When love beckons to you, follow him,*
> *Though his ways are hard and steep.*
> *And when his wings enfold you yield to him,*
> *Though the sword hidden among his pinions may wound you.*
> *And when he speaks to you believe in him,*
> *Though his voice may shatter your dreams as the north wind lays waste the garden.*

It is my hope and prayer that this narrative will offer comfort to others who may be vilifying themselves, living amid the same fog of guilt and confusion that we did for so long. Even if it helps just one person, it will be worth it. This is not to say that I encourage people to engage in GA relationships free from self-conscious responsibility, or even guilt. On the contrary. I now see the problematic and, in some respects, pathological nature of our relationship. I see how inappropriate it was for me to be so enamoured by my birth father. At the core of my decision to share our story is a responsibility to raise awareness of GA so that proper warnings can be put in place by the medical, adoption and social services to help prevent these feelings developing out of control; and that leniency can be offered to anyone unfortunate enough to be caught by the law for engaging in a relationship of which, ultimately, they have no control.

There is another book that inspired me to step up and help give this topic the attention it deserves. Barbara Gonyo, who you may recall from Chapter 16 when I stumbled across her name in a Perth library in 1995, published her own confessional memoir in 2011 called *I'm His Mother But He's Not My Son*. In it, she described the helplessness and shame of falling for him. I have admiration for her courage to put her real name to her story. Her continuous speaking out about the intensity of her attraction to him has opened up this subject for discussion more than anything else.

As part of my processing over the last decade, I contacted Barbara Gonyo's support group, Truth Seekers in Adoption and spoke to her personally. I remember her as compassionate and wise. It was a relief to hear the similarities of experiences and feelings from her own mouth. To talk directly to another human being, who had experienced the sheer power and magnetism of Genetic Attraction; who was intelligent yet as baffled by the power of it as we were, was reassuring. She told me that hundreds of others had shared similar stories in her group. It was comforting in some way that we weren't particularly unique. (Truth Seekers in Adoption is now renamed GeneticSexualAttraction.com and is an online forum).

Her experience wasn't exactly like mine. Barbara never became intimate with her son. Each individual GA story has different and complex dynamics that influence how it plays out. But I feel that if Michael and I had been able to read a book, written by someone who had experienced a dilemma even closer to ours than hers, when we were in the midst of our lonely turmoil, thinking we were the only ones going through this crazy emotional roller coaster, it would have given us comfort that we were not in some way deviant. More importantly, it may have given us strength and courage to make different decisions – perhaps to peel ourselves away from each other; to accept that we had these strong feelings, which are a common reaction to adoption, but that they were misdirected. Such a book could have perhaps guided us to love each other in a different, more familial way.

I now understand that when any of us humans find ourselves in unusual, emotionally challenging or unknown territory for which we are not prepared, we all do the best we can, within the limits of our emotional and spiritual maturity. Ultimately, we come through unchartered waters with deeper insights into ourselves and the wider human experience, greater maturity and more resources to face life's further challenges.

I was an immature woman, who did the best she could with her understanding of the world at the time - a woman whose formative years were influenced by subconscious feelings of abandonment. At 24, as an adoptee harbouring the unrecognised trauma of separation from my birth mother, I had a desire for deep connection, which I had missed, either consciously or unconsciously.

Ten years ago, I took a career diversion and trained as a child counsellor. This has given me a thorough understanding of the emotional and psychological impact that a severing of the early mother-baby union has. I am convinced that GA gets its potency from the interruption of this natural bonding process, not only with the mother but with other blood relatives. This upheaval is buried as an unmet need in the subconscious of a child, who sees itself as relinquished and cast adrift from its biological roots. These needs forever call to be met so that the individual can feel whole. When a separated parent and child reunite as adults, their subconscious recreates this missed bonding process and it is often played out by falling uncontrollably in romantic love.

I sometimes envisage myself back in May 1965 as a newborn, ripped away from the fabric of all that I had known in my short life - the cosy genetic familiar within which my biological mother had enveloped me. I had been at one with her for nine months in the womb, and then surrounded by her smell, her voice and her touch for five weeks after birth. Then - in a flash - she was gone, and I was given to another 'mother'. How did that baby cope with that? I imagine it to be like a soul-split.

I've wondered if this formative experience has affected my entire interpretation of the world and my sense of belonging in it. As an infant, I couldn't risk being given away again and that's why my subconscious drove me to be 'as good as gold'. This is why, when I was growing up, all my parents' friends expressed what a 'good child' I was. This is perhaps why the day that I was dropped off at boarding school is the clearest childhood memory I have: It resembled another major separation experience.

When I met Michael, I experienced unconditional devotion for the first time. He met my craving for human closeness on every level. He loved me as a lover would, and protected me as a father would. He was my pillar of support when I couldn't carry on. I categorically knew that he would never leave me. This was in stark contrast to the wavering signals of security I received from my adoptive parents. Yes, they loved me, but I always felt I had to constantly earn their allegiance. 'This adoption is over,' are words they used several times during our hard times.

Michael's loyalty was indestructible in comparison. During all my yo-yoing between countries, his message was always, 'You must do what you want to do but I'm here for you whatever.' Like a parent allows a child their freedom but remains poised in the wings to lift them from peril, that's how he was with me. No other caregiver had truly done that.

However, over the years I have reflected deeply whether Michael had any culpability as the older, more responsible adult. 'Why didn't he stop?' is a question I have stalled on many times, and one which I expect will be on the mind of many readers.

In some of our heated exchanges during the years when my family tried to ostracise him, I shouted at him, 'You were older. You should have stopped it!' But he always reminded me that he was as naively blindsided by this unusual force of genetic attraction as I was.

All of us experience inappropriate attraction at some point. I know many people who've confessed that they've been caught off guard by an unspoken spark with a friend's partner; a rush of sexual chemistry with someone wildly younger; a secret crush on someone we know in a professional capacity. Most of us will also have experienced being consumed with love, or being spellbound by the power of attraction. There probably aren't many who can honestly say they did the right, sensible or wise thing when in its grip. With the biological force of genetic attraction on top, it was almost impossible for us to step away.

Let's not forget, Michael was shaped by his own difficulties in childhood. From a young age, he bore caregiving responsibilities for his younger siblings; then followed a crisis of confidence when he fell short of the high academic expectations put upon him; combined with undiagnosed dyslexia and ADHD; and to add insult to injury he was sent away to Australia by parents who made no secret of their exasperation at his lack of direction.

Reading more about the issues he faced, I have learned that for people with ADHD, the terrain of emotional and sexual relationships can be especially complex. ADHD affects impulse control, emotional regulation and how the brain experiences reward. People with this condition value immediate rewards more than the long-term consequences. Numerous studies have pointed to a higher likelihood for people with ADHD to have romantic or sexual relationships at younger ages; higher rates of unplanned pregnancies; or increased vulnerability to risky sexual behaviour. This isn't necessarily because they are unaware of risks, but because they have an exaggerated sense of the emotional or physical 'benefit' of activities. This is in part driven by dysregulation of dopamine, the hormone which impacts our motivation.

Added to this, many with ADHD will have experienced peer rejection or negative comments in early life, which can prime them for intense attachments later in life. This is not an excuse for having inappropriate relationships, nor is this to say that anyone with ADHD makes questionable relationship choices. But in Michael's case, these factors – a drive to connect, and a struggle to balance impulse and emotion with consequence - does go some way to explaining why he may have blurred the lines with our genetic attraction.

We are all shaped by our childhood experiences, no matter how insignificant they may seem. Our relationship with our caregivers dictates our attachment style. In psychology, elements that contribute to the development or worsening of a state or condition are known as 'morbidity factors'. Michael and I had lots of them! For me, there was adoption, a lack of preunion counselling, childhood wounds creating a need for love and approval; For

Michael, his struggles with undiagnosed ADHD were no doubt exasperated further by the guilt he carried for being unable to support Janet and preventing their child being given away to the unknown. Neither of us had a partner or spouse in the background to notice the intensity of the relationship and to gently question it.

Our relationship offered something which spoke to each of our deep-seated needs to be liked. For me, Michael was an older man who fully saw me. For him, I was a young alluring girl whom he could tell his ego he was saving. Yes, he was my father but only on paper – we had no family heritage.

If we were not carrying the weights of our past, we could have recognised that this was a dangerous arena and would have put the brakes on. Many people do meet a relative and experience a forbidden attraction, but do not follow through on it because they are more secure in themselves.

This leaves the second ultimate question: Do I regret what happened?

I have to answer, no. For all the pain, my relationship with Michael did open my heart and mind, helping me to see my own innate potential. For all the inappropriateness, I have been able to experience the true belonging that all humans crave, but which sadly alludes most of us for a lifetime. For all the legal complications, what endures is the memory of a potent, alchemical fusion of unconditional love and a profound recognition of our reflected selves. When we were together it was intoxicating – a current I couldn't resist. If I'm honest, I still miss that feeling. It is a paradox that while I would now recoil from those same dynamics, I long for that feeling of being cherished and utterly safe in his presence. There was no criticism of the other; no need to change or justify. Just a rare and complete acceptance.

But I don't want to paint a misleadingly rosy picture. The stress it had on my adoptive parents was immense. They felt they were losing their daughter. Yes, they treated Michael dreadfully, and yes, they said venomous things to me. But in their defence, they had no idea about the addictive potential of GA relationships nor the underlying traumas that drive adoptees into such relationships. They had always believed that if their baby was loved, it did not matter that she was adopted. The baby wouldn't know the difference. The only preadoption literature they were given was a book called *Yours by Choice,* which simply advised them on their commitment as adopting parents. They had no reason to believe that their baby may have suffered internally with her sense of belonging and identity. They saw what happened between Michael and me as black and white. He was older - a successful businessman, who should have known better. I was young and vulnerable and was being led astray. Over the years we did make a degree of peace with the past but our relationship always remained tenuous. I gave up hope of them ever understanding how adoption deeply impacted me, and they in turn accepted that the past happened and they cannot punish anyone for it. We no longer talk about anything to do with Michael.

Then there is the damage that our relationship did to Michael's life. After he was sentenced for incest, he was never really the same man. Not only did he lose me – the love of his life and his son – his ultimate joy, but he also nearly lost his career. Not to mention the huge financial toll in defending his name.

It is because of this damage to those closest to me that the urge to raise awareness of GA grew stronger. In 2010, I summoned the courage to take part in a TV documentary about relatives who have had relationships. The resulting title had the word 'incest' in it – presumably to grab attention - which I didn't know would be the case when I agreed to participate. The term incest often implies abuse of children, and I hated this being associated with GA relationships. Still, it provided a meaningful opportunity to shed light on the misunderstood concept of GA and the people from all walks of life who find themselves caught up in it.

My participation, which I did anonymously, led to an interview on a mainstream TV chat show, in which my voice and appearance were disguised. The host congratulated me for having the courage to talk about our relationship. The show's regular agony aunt also featured in the interview, and said the subject desperately needed talking about so that GA and incest don't get boxed up together any longer. She said that in the pre-show research, the production team had heard from several blood relatives, mainly brothers and sisters, who had fallen in love and then been hounded by the police.

When I first set about documenting my story, I thought it would be virtually impossible to explain it in a way that could accurately convey the total love and completeness that Michael and I felt together, while also not setting ourselves up to be morally judged. I will always remember that first beautiful hot sunny day we spent together - outside a pub, on the green, talking as if we'd somehow never been apart; how the chatter and laughter gave me a warmth and happiness that felt so familiar, yet so confusing; how the connection between us was almost tangible, yet we were so unsure how to deal with it. But today, approaching my sixtieth year, I have moved beyond fear that we will be misunderstood. I have faith that our story can stir up a measure of compassion for people like us, who have faced cruel judgements of law or moral condemnation about a GA relationship.

I can totally understand how hearing our story second hand, without knowledge of the characters involved; without acknowledgment of the traumas and guilt we each carried, could lead to a default position of judgement. But I hope that now I have told my story wholly, truthfully and within the context of the academic recognition of GA, it will be understood.

I know our story will still offend some people. It is for this reason that I choose to write under a pseudonym and why I have changed names, identifying details and exact dates of some events in this book. One of the main challenges for us as human beings is not to stand in judgement of others. I hope that my experiences, told from the heart, will help to replace judgement with empathy.

I'm also sharing it because so many love stories are woven with guilt, misunderstandings and retribution. Only in the last few years, through deep soul searching, meditation, reading and loving chats with my loyal friends, I have been able to quell the guilt that I did something wrong, to love and forgive myself, and thus begin to heal.

People caught up in GA relationships - or indeed other relationships which are forbidden by nature – are enslaved to intoxicating evolutionary forces. It takes courage to walk away.

In writing my story, I wanted to strike a delicate balance between giving those affected permission to forgive themselves, yet also advocating that they take appropriate responsibility. The choice to engage in a forbidden relationship is usually not in the best interests of the people in it, nor for those around them.

In that respect, this book acknowledges and commends the bravery that is necessary, yet so challenging, to renegotiate an inappropriate relationship and invest elsewhere romantically. But also it offers sympathy and invites self-compassion for those who find themselves drawn to a forbidden relationship through no fault of their own.

Epilogue

2025

Until 2025, I never dared return to Australia because of the warrant for my arrest. However, after Lucas decided to move there to join his beloved brother, my desire to return to be near them became too strong to put off any longer. True to my affirmation to face my fears, I made plans for my grand move. My instinct told me it would be ok, even though Michael discouraged me, fearing that my arrest on arrival could bring the whole saga back into the media.

I couldn't afford a lawyer so I my intention was to set off and face the music on arrival, surrendering to what was meant to be. When Michael realised that I was serious, at the 11th hour, he paid for a lawyer to look into my situation and advise accordingly.

The lawyer did whatever lawyers do behind the scenes and just days before I was due to fly, she reported in to say she had negotiated with the authorities that I would not be arrested on arrival, provided I agree to present myself at a police station at a date set by them. I was to provide her with the address where I would be staying (which was with James), and await further instructions once I arrived in the country.

Off I flew, leaving behind the life in Weston-super-Mare that I had built for more than two decades. My heart was in my chest as I walked through customs. I handed over my passport and seemingly nothing flagged up. I watched the passport controller's face intensely, scanning for any signs that she had detected something unusual. There was nothing. When the stamp pressed down and I was waved through, it felt momentous.

Weeks went by before I heard anything. Eventually, a phone

call from my lawyer arrived. Her voice sounded upbeat. 'I have positive news,' she revealed. My heart leapt. Maybe I'd been let off already! But it wasn't quite that simple. She had uncovered a file from the time of Michael's incest charges and found a *nolle presequi* statement (an instruction to not proceed with trial). She didn't know why it was there, but it meant that she had good grounds to appeal to remove the record entirely. She put a case together pointing out that the relationship happened many years ago; that I was now 59 years old; and that I had presented myself willingly to face the charges.

There was just one catch. While the case was ongoing, I would not be able to work with children.

I'd spent so long retraining as a child counsellor, which felt like my true calling, so I was not prepared to acquiesce on that. Not to mention that I needed an income! I went against her advice and proceeded with my application for clearance to work with minors. I wrote down my whole story in an evocative statement. James and Lucas poured over it with me for hours, redrafting and tweaking. Once we were satisfied with our heartfelt letter, I rang the body overseeing the security checks. I found myself pouring out my story to him and crying. He listened with patience and told me to send in my letter, addressed to him, and he would fast track it to head office.

The very next day, the same official phoned me personally and revealed that I was cleared to work with children! I cried, and later that evening I celebrated with champagne with James and Lucas. I was able to apply to a job which I had had my eye on for weeks, at a top clinic in town. Two weeks later, I got the job!

Meanwhile, my criminal case was not yet over. Weeks stretched out and I had not heard anything. It was almost six months after my arrival in the country that I was finally notified of a date to show up at a police station. James accompanied me to the door and then waited in a café while I was photographed and fingerprinted. The policewoman assigned to do all this soon got a sense of me, and likely realising that I was far from the profile of a typical criminal, she dropped her austere front and started sharing funny anecdotes about the other suspects who had passed through their doors that day.

'We would like to speak to the son you had from this relationship,' she said, becoming serious again.

'Sure, he's in a café down the road waiting for me. Shall I tell him to come now?' I replied without batting an eyelid.

She paused, gave a brief sigh before saying, 'You know what, love? That won't be necessary. You're free to go and we'll be in touch with your lawyer.'

My only condition of bail was to have no contact with my so-called 'co-offender' - Michael. I had to completely cut him off for three months. He found this hard to take seriously and kept calling and texting me. It was difficult not to respond, but I adhered strictly to the stipulations of my bail.

At long last, I received a date to appear at a magistrate court. But it was a Wednesday – a day when I was supposed to be working in the therapy centre. I was now only a week into the job. There was no way I could explain why I needed a day off! I called my lawyer and begged her to attend on my behalf.

'This is not a service I offer. I have never done that for any of my clients.' She told me assertively. I pleaded with her, and to my huge gratitude, she agreed! Aside from fearing losing my job, I was petrified of appearing in court and answering to a judge.

As more weeks passed, my quiet confidence that all would be ok started to waver. Why the delay? What if I wasn't cleared? Would I never again work with children? It was a haunting reminder of the familiar anxiety which I had lived with for so many years, and a window into what Michael suffered years earlier when he faced the courts.

Then, in late summer 2025, an unexpected email appeared in my inbox. The subject line: *Sophia, it's over.*

I clicked to find a forwarded message from my lawyer. It was full of jargon I did not understand, but I knew from her smiley face that it was the finale. My charge for incest was officially dropped. It was found to be a victimless crime.

***

I am now fully enjoying life in Australia, living near my sons and carving a niche in my career in the area that I'm most passionate about – the mother-baby bond. As a child counsellor, I bring in all the holistic skills I've acquired over my varied career including massage therapy; mindfulness meditation; clinical training as a physiotherapist. I show my clients how to tune in to their baby's needs in the first two years of life. In particular, the powerful benefits of breastfeeding, eye contact, skin-to-skin touch, mirroring and body language to foster a secure attachment style. Key to my approach is the need to demonstrate to a baby what love is and how love *feels*. This is paramount for any human's healthy emotional and psychological development. We all want to love and be loved; it's the driving force of the human heart. The way we learn to express love, as well as receive it, comes from how we were shown love in our tender early years.

I have not married and while I have loved again, I don't have a significant partner. I am still firm friends with Andrew and he remains a loving and supportive father to the boys.

Since my charges were dropped, I was able to resume communication with Michael. Our love has moved well beyond any romantic expression and is well and truly in the realm of the familial.

As for my birth mother, we resumed contact years after our fallout in 1990 and she now knows about the GA relationship. In fact, she heard my interview on the TV show by chance, and even though my voice and face were disguised, she had a hunch it was me. When she first learned the truth, she went through a myriad of emotions. She too, not surprisingly, wanted to blame Michael and expressed animosity towards him. But her abiding love for me meant that over time she came to accept and understand what happened. My half brother and sister – now adults - also know the truth and the sentiments they have offered have been a touching mix of love, compassion and forgiveness, as they have also come to understand the complexity of emotions that led to our unconventional union.

Finally, onto the most important anchors in my life - my two sons. They are blossoming as adults. They are kind, intelligent, strong, ambitious men happily exploring their passions and chosen careers. They are the best of friends despite long periods of separation. Against the odds, their love and high regard for each other has deepened and they are there for each other through thick and thin.

Both boys are spiritual and interested in the esoteric side of life. They are peacekeepers who care deeply about planet earth and a sustainable future. I often recall that mysterious man in the crystal shop in 1996 when James was two, who told me that he was here as my teacher. Then the subsequent visit to a psychic, who premonished that he would one day speak at the UN. I wouldn't be surprised if one day that came to pass. He has always been emotionally mature beyond his years, with insights that constantly move people around him.

He definitely inherited his father's poetic gene, with equal flare. I would like to end this book by sharing one of my favourite poems from James's collection. He wrote it for me on my birthday a few years ago. It moves me to tears every time I read it because it is spoken from his heart, testament to his love and appreciation of our mother-son relationship, despite what we have endured.

How could I regret having James?! If Michael and I hadn't had the courage - albeit wavering courage - to at least give our love a chance, despite the fear of condemnation, he would not be here. He has been nothing but a blessing and a joy to us both since the day he arrived in this world.

<u>Mother</u>
I've known you since before we met,
When time had not yet touched me.
I couldn't wait to start my life,
And meet my soul's new family.

When day one came to start the game,
And I opened up my eyes,
You were there, a gentle giant so loving, safe and wise.

A kind and young and happy lady,
Who'd been on her own journey,
What love and lessons you would give to this curious little baby.

You'd be the one to take my hand, and be there day and night,
And when the dark in life alarmed me,
You'd be the shining light.

As I grew and saw the world,
And tested the horizons,
You met my joy and tears and questions with never ending kindness.

My heart and mind grew strong and glad,
And steady in myself.
Your love showed me to put fear and doubt upon the shelf.

So this for you my darling mother I endeavour to direct,
A clear and loving message,
In which I declare your sons respect.

We will remember mothers love and its bright and gentle power,
For it's what makes the lotus bud become the lotus flower.

Addendum: Genetic Sexual Attraction - Psychology and The Law

Having taken it upon myself to research GSA, I'd like to share what I have learned about the historical and psychological theories, independently of my own subjective experiences that I've so far relayed. Even though I choose to use the term GA (Genetic Attraction) rather than GSA (Genetic Sexual Attraction) for reasons I've already stated in this book, for this chapter I use the two terms interchangeably because many of the academic and public references use the term GSA.

In the summer of 2015, I went to meet an anthropologist at UCL, Professor Roland Littlewood, who published peer-reviewed research on GSA in 1995 along with his colleague Maurice Greenberg, a former advisor to the Post Adoption Centre. Their study, *Post-adoption incest and phenotypic matching: Experience, personal meanings and biosocial implications*, covered 40 adoption cases, and eight extensive interviews. From this report and Greenwood's other clinical work at the Post Adoption Centre, they found a staggering 50% of people involved in post adoption reunions experienced strong sexual attraction.

Fifty percent is huge. I contacted Professor Littlewood after hearing of this research and met him in London. He listened with empathy to my story. He explained to me that Genetic Sexual Attraction can be explained by the Westermarck Effect Hypothesis. This idea is that humans have a kind of built-in 'safety mechanism' which protects us from feeling sexually attracted to family members, providing we grow up together before the age of six. Professor Littlewood has remained in contact with me since this meeting.

The Westermarck Effect Hypothesis is so named after the Finnish anthropologist Edvard Westermarck, who proposed the theory as an explanation for why incest is considered ubiquitously taboo in his book, *The History of Human Marriage* in 1891.

There is another fascinating piece of research from Israel in 1983 by Joseph Shepher, which appears to back up the Westermarck theory. Shepher's study, *Incest: A Biosocial View*, which is summarised in his book, *A Biosocial View* (1983), looked at marriage patterns of children reared in Kibbutz communes, who had sibling-*like* relationships but were not biologically related. Out of nearly 3,000 marriages, only 14 were between children from the same peer group. Of those 14 couples, none had been reared together during the first six years of life.

The Westermarck effect theory may seem to conflict with Freud's well-established doctrine from 1913 that all infants have sexual urges towards their opposite sex parent (widely known as the Oedipus Complex). Freud hypothesised that these feelings are so strong that they need to be repressed but that they get resolved between the ages of three to five, providing that they have a loving, non-traumatic relationship with parents. If the relationship isn't healthy then the child can develop neurosis and can have problems in the development of their 'superego', which acts as our moral compass through life.

Many other studies have since supported the notion that people tend to fancy parental lookalikes. For example, three experiments, conducted in 2010 by Chris Fraley of the University of Illinois and Michael Marks of New Mexico State University, found participants rated faces as more sexually attractive after subliminal exposure to the opposite sex parent's face or when faces were (unknowingly) morphed with their own. The effect reversed when the kinship was made explicit.

Although Littlewood and Greenwood's study is now more than thirty years old, it is still the most heavily cited. There was, however, a more recent study which built on their findings, suggesting that the Westermarck hypothesis is only one part of this 'safety mechanism' against incest. *Beyond Westermarck: Can Shared Mothering or Maternal Phenotype Matching Account for Incest Avoidance?* by Dr David Livingstone Smith concluded that there are at least two competing explanations as to why incest is so rare. One is the 'Maternal Phenotype Matching Hypothesis' – when we encounter someone new, we instantly but unconsciously scan their face to compare it to our mother's 'phenotype', thus checking it isn't too similar (which could indicate a genetic connection); The other is the 'Shared Mother Hypothesis' – when a child experiences or witnesses a mother nurturing a baby, it serves as a powerful signal of their 'mother-child' dynamic and rules them out as a potential romantic partner.

Clearly, the origins and triggers for GA are contested. Some psychologists propose that it's an unconscious attempt to reconstitute the bonding which should have happened between parent and newborn, or siblings. Then there is another speculative view from geneticists that romantic feelings could be dictated by the presence of unconsciously detected pheromones. I believe it's a combination of many things, and there is much scope for further research.

I would also like to understand what happens on a neurological level. Do oxytocin or serotonin levels change when DNA relatives reunite in a way that might compare to when people are in romantic love? There is good evidence to suggest that the reward-related neurochemicals like dopamine and oxytocin are ignited in similar ways when a mother breastfeeds her baby as when people are in early-stage romantic love.

What is clear is that GA requires more mainstream acknowledgment. Despite creeping awareness by adoption agencies, a few academics like Littlewood and Greenberg, and the odd sympathetic judge, there is no mention of it in The Diagnostic and Statistical Manual of Mental Disorders (DSM-5), which is considered the handbook by mental health professionals around the world, and which is often referred to in legal cases as proof that some actions are beyond our human control.

What fascinates me about GA is that it strikes normal people from all walks of life. Mother-son, mother-daughter, father-daughter, brother-sister, uncle-niece. All succumb to a feeling of overwhelming triumph - akin to finding the missing piece of a jigsaw they've been seeking all their lives. It is ubiquitous around the world. It cuts across all differentiates of age, class, culture and sexual orientation. In Professor Littlewood's study, two sisters, who had never previously expressed as lesbian, had a sexual affair.

In the literature I've read about GA - some academic, some media interviews, and some personal accounts on forums or social media - the common denominator is the fervour in the language used to describe how GA gripped them.

I've read it being described as a heaven and hell; A magnetic force of which you have absolutely no control; Like an affair, only with many more layers of complexity via moral conflicts, social conflicts, role conflicts, relationship conflicts and attachment-separation conflicts; Like you have met a part of yourself; Like you are talking to yourself or a mirror image - one you never knew about or could understand before; Absolutely uncontrollable; Like a Venus flytrap, sucking you in so you can't escape; Like being hit by a bolt of lightning, which causes the most sensible or intelligent people to behave in a way completely out of character.

Professor Littlewood explained to me something else called 'mirroring', which his co-author, Maurice Greenberg had encountered in his clinical work with the Post Adoption Centre. Mirroring is the shock of self-recognition. Reuniting relatives may spot shared features, mannerisms or traits and which add to the sensation of reconnection. It feels like they belong to each other in a special way. This resonated with me because I remembered how I froze when I first saw Janet and my stepbrother and stepsister on our first meeting near Luton airport. I'd never met anyone who resembled me before. This is why I feel that physical similarities are particularly powerful in Genetic Attraction; adopted people often have never met anyone who shares a distinct facial or bodily feature.

Genetic Attraction is like a rolling stone gathering moss. Because of the instant draw, people feel compelled to open up. They then embark on a crash course of learning about each other. There is a no-holds baring of souls, in a bid to catch up to the now. This honesty makes them feel even more like soulmates and results in a desire to cement this fervent connection with sexual intimacy. They just want to smell each other and touch their hair and get as physically close as possible. As adults, there is no more expressive way to execute this craving for closeness than sexual intimacy. Sexual fulfilment is the zenith of emotional synchronicity.

It seems to me that no amount of worldliness or emotional stability gives anyone the power to stop it. People affected by Genetic Attraction repeatedly point out that when they met as adults for the first time, they didn't feel the 'incest taboo' of our culture, because they didn't feel like father-daughter / brother-sister. Why? Because they met *as adults*. I recall once one of my family members suggesting that they could set me up with a cousin as a date. I was absolutely repulsed by the idea. My cousin! It is not the closeness of DNA which is the deterrent to romance, but the familiarity experienced as prepubescent youngsters.

Thankfully. since Greenberg and Littlewood's research, GSA has been included in the Adoption Practice Guide – a document given to people who work either as intermediaries or counsellors in the adoption community. The guide, produced jointly by Adoption England and the Department for Education, and informed by PAC-UK, the UK's largest adoption intermediary agency, includes a good couple of pages on GSA and cites the 50% figure mentioned in Greenwood's research. It acknowledges that there is no 'clear pathway' to help people reframe inappropriate feelings, but that a warm non-judgmental environment, advice, information, moral guidance and the reassurance that feelings are not unusual are all things which can help.

While the inclusion of this guidance is a huge leap from my

experience of being handed the phone number of my birth mother and sent on my way, mention of GSA is still not a set agenda item in pre-union counselling. There may still be many adoptees who don't hear about it because they don't bring it up with their counsellor or case worker. Some commentators have pointed out that because of the revulsion and stigma baked into the topic, the condition still remains obscure or ignored by professionals, and avoided as a topic of study by academics.

It's also been raised that this failure to tackle GSA head-on could become a problem for people conceived by donor eggs or sperm. You will recall from my own story that the changes in adoption laws in the mid-1970s gave adopted children the right to obtain a copy of their birth certificate. This is what allowed me to approach an adoption agency and for them to do the necessary research to trace my birth mother. Unsurprisingly this led to an increase in the number of reunions between adoptees and their blood relatives in the last few decades.

Similarly, new laws for donor-conceived people came into effect in April 2005, allowing them to find out the identity of their sperm or egg donor when they reach 18. This 'Removal of Anonymity Law' came about after studies carried out on adopted and donor-conceived children found that they benefitted emotionally from knowing their biological heritage.

Yet there is even less of a framework for counselling for children conceived through IVF. Meetings can be arranged casually via social media. Speaking to The Guardian in 2003, Sue Cowling, then deputy director of the Post-Adoption Centre warned, 'Genetic sexual attraction associated with IVF births is a time bomb waiting to go off.'

There is one positive development in the adoption world though, and that is the advocacy of open adoption. Open adoption is when birth parents and adoptive families maintain regular in-person contact. If relatives just exchange letters and photos, it is considered indirect contact, not 'open adoption', because sometimes letters are redacted or written in a way which does not disclose identifying details. Open adoption has been commonplace in the US for decades but has been less encouraged in the UK until recently.

Not only has there been a growing body of research on the benefits of ongoing contact for an adoptee's sense of identity and for accessing vital medical and cultural history; but the prevalence of social media has meant that the adoption community has had to confront the reality that many adoptees try to track relatives online. There has been a wave of adoptee-led advocacy on social platforms like TikTok, Instagram, and podcasts challenging the secrecy of traditional adoption. The result is a growing recognition among professionals that openness is a necessary adaption.

Interestingly, open adoption was actually the norm in the UK and the US until around the 1950s. Then, birth and adoption records were left unhidden. It was only due to the cultural stigma attached to unmarried mothers born in the 1950s and continuing into the 1960s – the era when Janet was unfortunate enough to get pregnant - when adoptions became closed again.

The other reason that Genetic Sexual Attraction needs to be better understood by the wider public is that currently there is no distinction in law between GSA and incest. Michael found this out when police said they were charging him with 'technical incest'. We later learned that there is no difference between 'incest' and 'technical incest' – this choice of phrase was likely used by the officer in question because mine and Michael's relationship didn't fit the stereotype of an abusive incestuous relationship. In their eyes we just fitted the 'technical' definition.

GA is distinct from incest because of the crucial factor of consent. It needs to be acknowledged and responded to differently in the frame of law. I am sure that all those who share my genetic attraction experience would agree that even the most successful of relationships rarely begin with such profound, spontaneous and mutual magnetism.

Whenever a story involving GA appears in the media, it is usually because the couple involved face criminal charges. Two cases in question are that of brother and sister, Patrick and Susan

Stübing in Germany. They grew up apart but met as adults, fell in love and had four children. Despite no evidence of neglect, all four children were taken into care. The brother served more than two years in prison for incest. Despite what they went through, the sister, when asked by a Guardian journalist in 2007 if she felt remorse, she apparently shook her head and said: 'No, I just want us to be able to live together.'

Another prominent case is that of reuniting brother and sister, Allen and Patricia Muth, in the US. Patricia was raised in care and did not meet her brother until she was 18. Their case went to the Supreme Court in 2005. Both pleaded not guilty to incest but still served prison sentences.

You will also recall the case of John and Jenny Deaves, which Michael insisted his lawyers use in his defence when fighting charges of incest. Their story manifested as lurid headlines such as this one in The Mirror, *My husband ran off with his daughter – then came home and said it was best sex ever.* They escaped judicial sentences but had their children taken into care temporarily – an ordeal both distressing and humiliating for all.

Such insensitive handling of cases shows a total lack of understanding of the nuance of GA. Pam Hodgkins, founder and former CEO of what used to be NORCAP – an adoption support group, warned in an interview with The Guardian newspaper 20 years ago, 'If the laws are not re-examined to take into account the complexities faced by reunited adults, society is simply going to have to become more tolerant of such relationships because they are not going to go away.'

Currently, the laws on incest vary across the world. The only universal is that all countries prohibit full sibling or parent–child marriages. But some countries, like the Netherlands, France, Slovenia and Spain don't criminalise consensual sexual relations between lineal relatives and siblings – they just ban marriage. First cousin marriage is legal in many western countries, including most of Europe and is even common in some cultures. But bring in aunt or uncle relations and the rules vary again. Sweden is the only country that allows marriage between half siblings as long as they get government permission.

Despite there being well documented evidence that GA is a real and prominent danger for adoptees and their birth parents; and despite legal precedents like the case of the Deaves, where the judge acknowledged there was no coercion; the relationship dynamics are still tip-toed around by professionals, and still incorrectly lumped together with incest in the eyes of the law and an easily shocked public.

There needs to be a paradigm shift. The law should not punish people simply for succumbing to a need or a feeling stirred in them so deeply that it rocks the core of who they thought they were. The way to protect people from heartbreak, psychological torment and the unforgiving law is through education and support.

The powerful hold of Genetic Sexual Attraction may remain mysterious, but it is a real and irresistible force which human will alone stands little chance to fight. Now I have experienced first-hand how strong this cocktail is, I feel strongly that people need to be protected from it. Ever since I discovered this concept tucked away in that little library in a Perth suburb, it started to dawn on me how different my life may have been if I'd been warned about it.

If, in those early days living in the dormitory accommodation, when I longed for the telephone to ring with Michael's voice, a professional had said to me, 'If you have romantic notions, remember who you are. Come and talk to us,' maybe we would have been able to establish a relationship that was more like that of father and daughter.

By the time we heard about the phenomenon of GA, the expression of our love had gone way beyond father and daughter, and so the discovery of GA didn't invalidate our love or disperse our feelings. There was nothing to help us understand how on earth two sincere, well-meaning people ended up in a situation that brought such isolation, cruel judgements of law, vicious inter-family rows and a visceral fear of moral condemnation.

Perhaps if I'd known about GA, I might have navigated my emotions differently. Perhaps I wouldn't have gone to Australia. Perhaps I would have taken that position as a tutor at the beauty academy where I trained. Perhaps I would have married Sean and raised three children with the same father. But we'll never know. Some questions belong to a past that cannot be altered.

I no longer linger on what might have been. My hope now is that by illuminating a subject many find uncomfortable, it may be met with empathy rather than judgement; that others who walk a similar path may find understanding instead of shame, and never have to carry the same regrets or quiet sorrow that we have.

Gadfly Press hopes that you have enjoyed this book, and we appreciate you taking the time to leave an Amazon review!

Acknowledgements

This book has not been an easy story to tell and could not have been written without the love, strength and encouragement of many people.

To my sons, whose love has been a constant light in my life - you have given me the courage to keep going, even in the most difficult moments. Everything I have overcome, I have done with you in my heart.

To Andrew, who came into my life with an open heart and chose to understand a story that was not easy to hear. Your love, steadiness and quiet strength have been a constant source of support and grounding.

As a devoted father to our son and a caring committed presence in my first borns life, you have given more than I could ever have asked for.

Your acceptance, compassion and unwavering support have meant everything to me - without you, I truly do not know where I would be today.

My sincere thanks to Professor Roland Littlewood for his insight, compassion and willingness to engage with this complex and sensitive subject, and for shedding light for me on the implications of the absence of the usual biological protection we all take for granted – known as the Westermarck Effect.

I am deeply grateful to my ghost writer who helped me shape this story and find the words to express what has often felt impossible to say.

To the friends who stood beside me, who listened without judgement, and who encouraged me to tell this story - you know who you are, and I will always be thankful.

Finally, to those whose lives have been touched by similar experiences, I hope this book helps you feel less alone.

An adoption story published by Gadfly Press and available worldwide on Amazon!

Blue Plastic Cow: One Woman's Search for Her Birth Mother

By Barbara Attwood

This is the true story of Barbara's adoption by a family who lived in a town on the banks of the River Mersey. They were a loving family but Barbara always felt different. Her mother, Florrie, never wanted her to know the truth. At age 12, after Barbara accidentally discovered that she was adopted, Florrie lied to her about her birth mother, Carole, and the facts surrounding her birth.

As a teenager, unable to deal with the shock of what she'd learned, she rebelled against her parents, finding solace in the exciting 1960s' Liverpool music scene. Against her parents' wishes, she got a job in Liverpool as a secretary. She went to lunch time sessions at the Cavern where she saw The Beatles, and often stayed out late in Liverpool drinking.

Decades later, Barbara discovered tear stained letters from her birth mother, containing heart-breaking words that would send her on a challenging 26-year quest to find Carole and discover the secret of the blue plastic cow.

www.ingramcontent.com/pod-product-compliance
Lightning Source LLC
LaVergne TN
LVHW020043110826
845155LV00029B/614